Business PLUS

Preparing for the workplace

Margaret Helliwell

CAMBRIDGE
UNIVERSITY PRESS

Student's Book **1**

CAMBRIDGE
UNIVERSITY PRESS

79 Anson Road, #06-04/06, Singapore 079906

Cambridge University Press is part of the University of Cambridge.

It furthers the University's mission by disseminating knowledge in the pursuit of education, learning and research at the highest international levels of excellence.

www.cambridge.org
Information on this title: www.cambridge.org/9781107640689

First published 2014

Printed in Singapore by C.O.S. Printers Pte Ltd

ISBN 978-1-107-64068-9 paperback Student's Book 1
ISBN 978-1-107-66880-5 paperback Teacher's Manual 1

Additional resources for this publication at www.cambridge.org/businessplus

Acknowledgments

The author and publisher thank the many teachers in the Asian region whose invaluable insights helped revise and fine-tune *Business Plus*. We would like to mention the following in particular:

Professor Hyojin Chung, Dongguk University, South Korea

Da-Fu Huang, Southern Taiwan University of Science and Technology, Tainan, Taiwan

Hsiu-Hui Su, Chaoyang University of Technology, Taichung, Taiwan

Gideon Hockley-Hills, SEIKO Inc., Osaka, Japan

Kelly Kimura, Soka University, Tokyo, Japan

Ms. Sirirat Poomprasart, University of the Thai Chamber of Commerce (UTCC), Bangkok, Thailand

The author's special thanks go out to Stuart Vinnie, Cambridge University Press Senior Training Consultant for the ASEAN region, whose experience of teachers' needs and teaching situations throughout Asia helped to mold her materials to best match the reality in the classroom, and on the editorial side, Chris Caridia, for his good ideas and endless patience. Last but not least, Bob Culverhouse and Ann Jobson for hours of patient listening!

The author would also like to thank the following Cambridge University Press regional staff for their support and advice, without which this course would never have been possible: Nuntaporn Phromphruk, Panthipa Rojanasuworapong and Sura Suksingh (Thailand); Ron Kim and Seil Choi (South Korea); Tomomi Katsuki, John Letcher, and David Moser (Japan); Irene Yang (Taiwan).

Book and cover design by Designers Collective
Book layout by Transnet Pte Ltd
Illustrations by Albert Design House, and Transmise Publishing Service
Casting and audio production by Voice Over Asia Co., Ltd

Plan of the book

Reading	Culture focus	Business writing	Learning outcomes
			Students can . . .
Talking about jobs	Meeting and greeting		■ welcome a visitor. ■ ask for and give personal information. ■ open, continue, and close a conversation. ■ ask for and tell people numbers. ■ talk about countries and regions. ■ understand a text about different jobs. ■ talk about greeting people in different countries.
Offices around the world		Emails	■ talk about different types of office. ■ describe an office and talk about routines. ■ ask about and describe a typical day. ■ talk about office equipment and where it is. ■ understand a text about different offices. ■ write an email to ask for information.
The unbreakable cell phone	Business cards in Asia		■ understand telephone phrases. ■ talk about what people are doing now. ■ understand telephone messages and talk about cell phones. ■ spell names. ■ use telephone language. ■ understand a text about new smartphones. ■ read a text about business cards in Asia.
Showrooming		An inquiry	■ understand conversations in a store. ■ use *some/any* and *much/many*. ■ talk about shopping habits and service in stores. ■ understand and give directions. ■ use words that go together. ■ understand a text about the future of shopping. ■ write an email asking for product information.
London to Beijing in two days	Communication styles		■ understand a conversation about making appointments. ■ discuss future plans. ■ understand a discussion about plans and make suggestions. ■ talk about times and dates. ■ understand the main idea of a text about future plans. ■ understand different communication styles.

Plan of the book

Reading	Culture focus	Business writing	Learning outcomes
			Students can . . .
The Richmond Hotel, Jakarta		A confirmation	<ul><li>change a hotel reservation on the phone.</li><li>compare people, places, and things.</li><li>talk about vacations and ways to travel.</li><li>use different words to talk about traveling.</li><li>describe pictures.</li><li>understand comments on a hotel.</li><li>write a confirmation email.</li></ul>
Top jobs for women	Conversation taboos		<ul><li>understand somebody talking about a company.</li><li>talk about things in the past.</li><li>research and present information about a company.</li><li>talk about countries and nationalities.</li><li>ask and answer questions with *make* and *do*.</li><li>understand a text about women in top jobs.</li><li>understand conversation taboos.</li></ul>
Special requests on MJets		Invitations	<ul><li>understand an invitation and a conversation in a restaurant.</li><li>use the modal verbs *can*, *must*, *have to*, *need to*.</li><li>use countable and uncountable nouns.</li><li>talk about a restaurant menu.</li><li>talk about food, drinks, and a favorite dish.</li><li>invite somebody and say yes or no to an invitation.</li><li>understand a text about a private jet service.</li><li>invite somebody and write yes or no to an invitation.</li></ul>
Tourists in Thailand	Body language in Asia		<ul><li>understand a conversation about work and leisure.</li><li>use *-ing* and *to*-infinitive forms after some verbs.</li><li>use connecting words.</li><li>understand and talk about travel and leisure in Asia.</li><li>talk about leisure time activities.</li><li>understand a text about tourism in Thailand.</li><li>understand body language in Asian countries.</li></ul>
The ASEAN Economic Community		A thank-you email	<ul><li>understand people saying goodbye.</li><li>use *will* and *won't* to talk about the future.</li><li>listen to and talk about life in the future.</li><li>say hello and goodbye and use prepositions after verbs.</li><li>understand an article about the advantages of the ASEAN Economic Community.</li><li>write a thank-you email.</li></ul>

Before you begin

Can you match the business situations in Units 1–10 with the photos? Then check the units.

1 **Nice to meet you**
At the airport

2 **In the office**
Types of office

3 **On the phone**
Can I take a message?

4 **Buying and selling**
Helping customers

5 **What are you doing tomorrow?**
Making an appointment

6 **Out and about**
Customer service in a hotel

7 **Tell me about your company**
The story of a company

8 **Let's eat out**
Entertaining in the business world

9 **Work and play**
During and after work

10 **Come again soon!**
Saying goodbye

Singapore

Osaka

Bangkok

Hiroshi

Nice to meet you

1 Business situation
At the airport

A) 〔1〕 **Hiroshi Akimoto works for GameZ, a video games company in Japan. He is at the airport to meet two visitors. Listen. Check (✔) what you hear.**

1 ☐ Excuse me.
2 ☐ No, I'm not.
3 ☐ Yes, that's right.
4 ☐ Good afternoon.
5 ☐ Welcome to Osaka.

6 ☐ This is my colleague.
7 ☐ Can I help you with your coat?
8 ☐ That's very kind.
9 ☐ How was your flight?
10 ☐ It was fine.

B) 〔1〕 **Listen again. Check (✔) true or false.**

	True	False
1 Mr. Akimoto and Mr. Tomlin know each other.		
2 Mr. Tomlin and Ms. Klein arrive in the morning.		
3 The airport is in Osaka.		
4 Ms. Klein is Mr. Akimoto's colleague.		
5 The flight was long and hard.		
6 Mr. Akimoto wants to take a taxi.		

C) **Work in groups of three. Practice meeting and introducing yourself and others.**

Excuse me. Are you . . . ?
My name is . . .
Nice to meet you.
Nice to meet you, too.
How was your flight / your trip?

Good morning/afternoon.
I'm . . . from . . .
This is . . .
Can I help you with . . . ?

▷ ▪ airport ▪ colleague ▪ flight
▪ to meet ▪ to introduce

I can welcome a visitor.

2 Grammar focus
The verb *to be* and the present simple

A Read the information about these four businesspeople.

	Hiroshi Akimoto	Lin Yao Chen	Christine Klein	Robert Tomlin
from	Tokyo, Japan	Taipei, Taiwan	Berlin, Germany	Glasgow, Scotland
works in	Osaka, Japan	Osaka, Japan	London, UK	London, UK
company	GameZ	GameZ	Digital Design	Digital Design
job	marketing manager	IT data scientist	video game designer	product manager

Hiroshi Akimoto and Lin Yao Chen are colleagues. They work for GameZ in Japan. What do they do there? Hiroshi is a marketing manager. Lin Yao is an IT data scientist. They like their jobs. They live in Osaka, but they don't come from there. Hiroshi comes from Tokyo. And where does Lin Yao come from? She comes from Taipei.

Christine Klein and Robert Tomlin are colleagues, too. But they aren't in the same department. Christine is a video game designer. Robert is a product manager. They work for Digital Design in London, but they don't live in London. They live outside London. And where do they come from? Robert comes from Glasgow and Christine comes from Berlin. She isn't English. She's German. But she doesn't speak German at work. She speaks very good English. And you? Do you speak good English, too?

He is a marketing manager. She is an IT data scientist.
We use *an* before the letters *a, e, i, o,* and *u.*

B Complete the chart. How many examples of these forms can you find in the text?

The verb *to be*		
Long form	**Short form**	**Negative**
he is		he isn't
she is		
	they're	

Hiroshi is a marketing manager.

C Complete the sentences.

Present simple	
Statements	
Hiroshi .... for GameZ. He .... his job. Lin Yao .... for GameZ, too. She also .... her job.	Hiroshi and Lin Yao .... for GameZ. They .... their jobs.
Negatives	
Christine comes from Berlin, but she .... there. Robert comes from Scotland, but he .... there.	Christine and Robert work in London, but they .... there.
Questions	
A: Where .... Lin Yao .... ? **B:** She works in Osaka. **A:** What .... she .... ? **B:** She's an IT data scientist.	**A:** Where .... Hiroshi and Lin Yao .... ? **B:** They work in Osaka. **A:** What .... they .... ? **B:** He's a marketing manager. She's an IT data scientist.

What do you do? asks about a person's job.

D Complete the chart.

Present simple	Positive	Negative	Questions
I/you/we/they he/she/it	work	.... doesn't	Do .... ? .... ?

E Work with a partner. Ask your partner five questions with *Do you . . . ?* Use these verbs: *work, like, live, come, speak*. Answer your partner's questions.

A: *Do you come from Osaka?*
B: *Yes, I come from Osaka. / No, I don't come from Osaka. I come from Bangkok.*

Over two and a half million people live and work in Osaka.

▷ ▪ company ▪ department ▪ marketing manager
 ▪ data scientist ▪ designer

I can ask for and give personal information.

A ▎2▎ **How do you start a conversation? The words in these sentences are mixed up. Put them in the correct order. Then listen and check.**

1 At a hotel
   A: me / excuse / Ms. Lee / are / you ?
   B: that's / yes / right / Mr. Tang / must / you / be
   A: am / I / yes / to / keep / you / sorry / waiting / I'm
   B: right / all / that's

2 On an airplane
   A: are / you / to / Indonesia / on / business / going ?
   B: I / yes / am / you / and ?
   A: no / on / vacation / going / I'm
   B: you / lucky !

B ▎3▎ **When we meet somebody for the first time, we often talk about everyday topics. Listen to the conversation and check (✔) the topics the two people talk about.**

☐ food   ☐ hobbies   ☐ jobs   ☐ language   ☐ traffic   ☐ vacations

What do you talk about in your country when you don't know somebody?

C ▎4▎ **Listen to two ways to finish a conversation. Complete the sentences.**

1 **A:** Well, it was .... to you.
   B: Yes, I hope .... sometime.
   A: That would be great. I'll call you next
       time I ....
   B: Fine.

2 **A:** Would you .... ? I have to go soon.
   B: What time .... leave?
   A: At six. So I really ....
   B: .... Shall I call you a taxi?

D **Work with a partner. Practice the conversations in 3A and 3C.**

▷ ▪ topics ▪ conversation ▪ excuse me
  ▪ on business ▪ on vacation

I can open, continue, and close a conversation.

Vocabulary focus
Focus 1: Numbers

A 〔5〕 Listen to the flight announcements and fill in the chart.

	Flight number	Destination	Gate		Flight number	Destination	Gate
1		Bangkok		**4**			
2				**5**			
3				**6**			

B 〔6〕 Complete the telephone messages with the numbers you hear.

1

To: _Mr. Akimoto_
From: _Robert Tomlin_
Message: _Please call at the Hilton in_
Osaka.
Number: _____

2

To: _Ms. Chen_
From: _Christine Klein_
Message: _She has some new_
information. Please call.
Number: _____

3

To: Ms. Otaka
From: Miti Arak, Palace Hotel
Message: Room is booked. Call if you
have questions.
Number: _____

4

To: _Yoshio Tani_
From: _Cintya Dewi_
Message: _Fax is working. Please_
send documents.
Number: _____

C Work with a partner. Ask your partner for these numbers.
Write the numbers down and then your partner can check them.

1 his/her age   ....
2 the age of two members of his/her family   ....
3 his/her house number   ....
4 his/her telephone number   ....

I can ask for and tell people numbers.

D **7** Listen and check (✔) the countries and regions you hear.

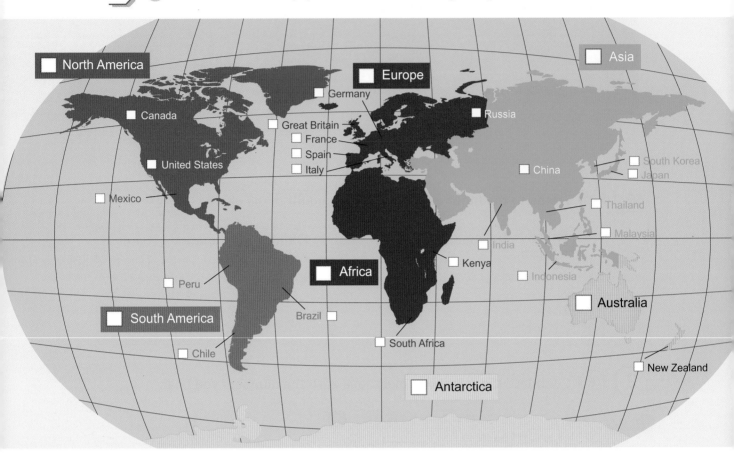

E Talking about ... countries and regions

Step 1: Work with a partner. List . . .

☐ five countries in Asia.   ☐ two countries in Africa.

☐ five countries in Europe.   ☐ two countries in South America.

☐ three countries in ASEAN.   ☐ two countries in North America.

Step 2: Form a small group and compare your lists.

F ▷ **Key words** Look at the words at the bottom of pages 1–4. Choose the best words to complete the sentences.

1 A lot of planes fly from this ....
2 Christine and Robert work together. She is his ....
3 Hiroshi works in the marketing ....
4 Christine is a video game ....
5 I'm not here on business. I'm here ....
6 We use everyday .... to start a ....
7 How was your ....?
8 .... Is this seat free?

I can talk about countries and regions.

Reading
Talking about jobs

A) **Before you read** You have three minutes to make a list of all the jobs you know. Then skim the article to see if the jobs it talks about are on your list.

Asian Business **Online**

talks to four young people in the ASEAN region about when they use English in their jobs.

My name is Tran Van Huan. I'm a computer specialist in Hanoi. I make computer networks for companies, and I train people to use the networks. I don't work for a company. I work for myself. I like my job. It's interesting. I work with companies all over the world, and we use English to communicate.

My name is Nadia Tengu. I'm a department manager in a bookstore in Kuala Lumpur. I wear a uniform, but only at work. I like my colleagues a lot. Our store is open every day, so we work very hard. Sometimes we have customers from China or Europe, and I need to speak English to help them.

My name is Cintya Dewi. I'm a website designer. I work in an electronics company in Jakarta. It's a big company, so I don't know everyone, only the colleagues in my department. We do a lot of business with Chinese and Indian firms, so I need to read and write emails in English.

My name is Miti Arak. I'm a hotel receptionist in Bangkok. I meet a lot of people in my job. Sometimes I work at night, but I don't like that very much. Most of our guests are from other countries, so we usually use English to communicate. Some of our staff also speak Chinese and German.

B) **Scanning for detail** Are the statements correct? If not, correct them.

Tran Van Huan	**1** . . . works for a company.
	He doesn't work for a company. He works for himself.
	2 . . . trains people in companies.
	3 . . . thinks his job is boring.
Nadia Tengu	**4** . . . works in Kuala Lumpur.
	5 . . . wears a uniform all the time.
	6 . . . works in a store that closes on Sundays.
Cintya Dewi	**7** . . . designs websites.
	8 . . . works in a small company.
	9 . . . knows all her colleagues in the company.
Miti Arak	**10** . . . works in a hotel.
	11 . . . meets a lot of people.
	12 . . . likes to work at night.

C) **Now you** Choose a person from your family and write about his or her job.

My brother is a(n) . . . He works in . . .   He likes/doesn't like his job because . . .

I can understand a text about different jobs.

6 Culture focus
Meeting and greeting

A Label the pictures with the greetings 1 to 8.

1 shake hands	**5** hug
2 kiss on the cheek	**6** bow
3 rub noses	**7** kiss on the hand
4 wai	**8** exchange business cards

B Which greetings are usual in your country for

1 family and friends? **2** business partners?

Do you know other greetings?

C In Europe and North America people usually shake hands when they meet. Here are some tips. Which is correct, A or B?

Tips for a correct handshake	
1 Use your **A** left hand. **B** right hand.	**3** When you shake hands, **A** look in a person's eyes. **B** don't look in a person's eyes.
2 Your handshake must be **A** strong, but not too strong. **B** very strong.	**4** A correct handshake is **A** quick. **B** for 30 seconds.

I can talk about greeting people in different countries.

In the office

1 Business situation
Types of office

A one-person office

B open-plan office

A In which picture can you see this, A or B?

- ☐ a lot of people
- ☐ a man alone
- ☐ family photos
- ☐ four desks
- ☐ a man without a jacket
- ☐ a man with a jacket
- ☐ an orange office chair
- ☐ telephones

B 🔊 8 Listen to Robert Tomlin and Lin Yao Chen talking about their different offices. Does Robert or Lin Yao say this? Put a check (✔).

	Robert	Lin Yao
1 It's quiet here.	✔	
2 There are 10 colleagues.		
3 There's no one to talk to.		
4 Colleagues want to chat.		
5 There's always a lot of noise.		
6 It's a bit noisy and hectic.		

C Complete each sentence with the correct word.

communicate	~~colleagues~~	desk
freedom	noise	noisy	waste

1 My *colleagues* are great people to work with.
2 It's easier to .... in an open-plan office.
3 I have a computer and a printer on my ....
4 You can .... a lot of time at work.
5 Be quiet! Don't make so much ....
6 My office isn't quiet. It's ....
7 Robert has more .... in a one-person office.

It's quiet in a one-person office.

▷ ▪ desk ▪ file cabinet ▪ hectic
▪ to waste time

I can talk about different types of offices.

Grammar focus

Focus 1: *There is . . . , there are . . .*

A 🔊 8 **Listen again to Robert Tomlin and Lin Yao Chen talking about their offices. Complete the sentences.**

1 .... a desk, a chair, and a file cabinet in Robert's office.
2 .... always a lot of noise in an open-plan office.
3 Lin Yao doesn't want a one-person office because .... no one to talk to.
4 .... 10 colleagues in Lin Yao's office.
5 In a one-person office, ... only four walls to look at.

B **Look at these sentences.**

A: **Is** there a printer in the office?   A: **Are** there any files in the office?
B: Yes, there is. **It** is on the desk.   B: Yes, there are. **They** are in the file cabinet.

What's the rule? Underline the correct word.

> Use *there is* with a **singular / plural** word.
> Use *there are* with a **singular / plural** word.

C **Work with a partner.**

Student A: Go to Partner file 1.
Student B: Look at the picture below.

You each have a picture of the same office, but on different days. There are 10 differences. Can you find them? Take turns to ask questions.

Is there a . . . in your picture?
Are there any . . . in your picture?
How many . . . ?
Where . . . ?
What color . . . ?

files	printer	plant
bookcase	desk	empty
full	lamp	calculator
notepad	trash can	

D **Use a word from each box to make sentences with *there are*.**

nine ten eleven ~~twelve~~ twenty-six thirty-one	countries days letters ~~months~~ planets players	English alphabet ASEAN January soccer team solar system year

There are twelve months in a year.

....

▷ ▪ noise ▪ bookcase
▪ printer ▪ difference

E (8) **Listen again and complete the sentences. Then put the words on the scale.**

1 You can .... waste a lot of time because colleagues want to chat.
2 There's .... a lot of noise.

100%   *always*
....
....
....
....
0%   *never*

~~always~~	not often	sometimes
~~never~~	often	usually/normally

F **Look at these sentences:**

I always get up early.   He is never late for work.
She often sends text messages.   The printer doesn't usually break down.

What's the rule? Underline the correct word.

Adverbs of frequency go **before / after** a full verb *(go, get, send . . .)*,
but **before / after** the verb *to be* and **before / after** *can, doesn't, don't.*

G **The words in these sentences are mixed up. Put them in the correct order.**

1 go / meetings / I / often / to / don't
2 time / is / Shaifful / on / never
3 always / colleagues / are / My / helpful
4 often / a / lunch / restaurant / don't / They / in / eat
5 his / always / birthday / Kamol / celebrates
6 emails / doesn't / many / get / usually / Hiroshi
7 They / on / summer / always / in / vacation / go / the

*I **never** give up!*

H **Interview a partner. Check (✔) the box that tells you about your partner.**

Are you ever late for class?   *Do you ever . . . ?*   *How often do you . . . ?*

	always	usually	often	sometimes	not often	never
be late for class	☐	☐	☐	☐	☐	☐
take taxis	☐	☐	☐	☐	☐	☐
eat street food	☐	☐	☐	☐	☐	☐
go to the movies	☐	☐	☐	☐	☐	☐
play computer games	☐	☐	☐	☐	☐	☐
go to bed after midnight	☐	☐	☐	☐	☐	☐

I **Tell the class.**

Kulap is never late for class. She sometimes eats street food, and she often goes . . .

▷ • to break down • to celebrate
  • midnight

I can describe an office and talk about routines.

3 Listening and speaking
A typical day

A ⑨ An interviewer asks three businesspeople about a typical day. Listen and complete the chart.

	Cintya	Mike	Kitty
1 What time do you get up in the morning?			
2 What time do you usually get to work?			
3 What is the first thing you usually do when you get to work?			
4 Where do you have lunch?			
5 How often do you travel on business?			
6 What do you do in the evenings?			

B Interview a partner about their typical day. Use these question words:

when	what	where	how often

C **Talking about ...** a day in the life of a famous person

Step 1: Work with a partner. Choose a famous person – a sports person, movie star, businessperson, etc.
What about . . . ? I think . . . is an interesting person.

Step 2: What do you think the person does on a typical day?
He/She usually gets up at . . .
He/She always has . . . for breakfast. After breakfast, . . .

Step 3: Work with another pair. Ask questions about their person.
What times does . . . ? When does . . . ?

Step 4: Tell the class who your famous person is and describe his or her typical day.

▷ ▪ cafeteria ▪ to spend time ▪ sales manager
▪ sales office ▪ tired

I can ask about and describe a typical day.

4 Vocabulary focus

Focus 1: Office equipment

A Label the things in the pictures with numbers 1 to 10.

1 stapler	3 hole punch	5 in-box	7 sales chart	9 markers
2 tape	4 paper clips	6 trash can	8 flash drive	10 folders

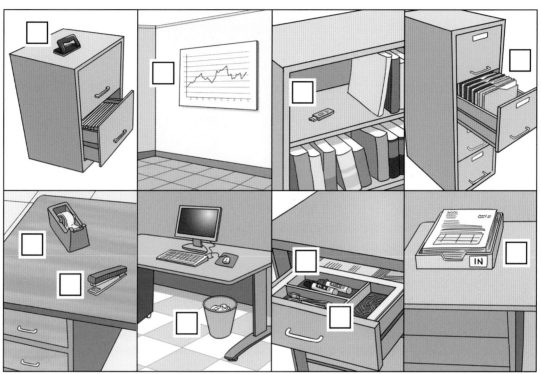

B Look at the pictures. Underline the correct preposition.

1 The hole punch is **on** / **in** / **under** the file cabinet.
2 The trash can is **under** / **on** / **in** the desk.
3 The in-box is **at** / **on** / **in** the desk.
4 The markers are **in** / **under** / **on** the drawer.
5 The flash drive is **in** / **on** / **at** the shelf.
6 The sales chart is **on** / **at** / **in** the wall.
7 The folders are **on** / **in** / **under** the file cabinet.
8 The paper clips are **in** / **on** / **under** the drawer.

C Look around your classroom and say what is in the room and where it is.

D Work with a partner. Read these conversations aloud.

A: Can I use your files?	A: Can I use your hole punch?
B: Sure. I don't need them right now.	B: Sorry. I need it right now.
A: Where are they?	A: OK. Thanks anyway.
B: They're in the file cabinet.	
A: Thanks.	

Write down four things in 4A that you need and four things you don't need.
Then have conversations with your partner.

Vocabulary focus

Focus 2: Words that go together (1)

E 🔊 9 **Listen to the interviews in 3A again. Match the words 1 to 8 with the words A to H.**

1	leave	**A**	the children
2	make	**B**	on business
3	turn on	**C**	for work
4	travel	**D**	in the office late
5	take care of	**E**	coffee
6	check	**F**	the fashion shows
7	stay	**G**	the computer
8	go to	**H**	my email

She leaves for work at eight.

F 🔊 9 **Listen to 3A again. Complete the sentences with the missing words.**

1 Tell us about your .... day.
2 Mike is a .... manager.
3 He always has lunch in the .... cafeteria.
4 In the evening Mike often has .... calls.
5 The .... office of Mike's company is in the US.
6 Kitty always .... work at nine.
7 There's a nice café just around the ....

G **Which of the words doesn't go with the word in green?**

1	quiet	office / day / person / noise
2	web	designer / site / book / address
3	ten	desk / colleagues / o'clock / emails
4	have	lunch / a meeting / coffee / night
5	on	business / morning / vacation / the telephone
6	waste	time / money / energy / telephones
7	at	my desk / six-thirty / business / work
8	make	coffee / an email / a mistake / a phone call

He usually makes coffee at work.

H ▷ **Key words** Look at the words at the bottom of pages 9–12. Choose the best word to complete the sentences.

1 The printer in the office often ....
2 Cintya likes to .... with her children.
3 I work hard, so in the evenings I'm always ....
4 We usually go to bed before ....
5 Our office isn't quiet. There's always a lot of ....
6 Do you usually .... your birthday?
7 Mike is a .... for an American company.
8 We can have lunch in the ....

I can talk about office equipment and where it is.

A **Before you read** Look at the pictures. Describe what you see.

Asian Business **Online**
looks at some of the coolest offices in the world.

More than 100 people from 31 countries work for the Mindvalley education company. The company believes that work should be fun, and so it has made a positive environment full of light and color. Every morning the workers can choose their own table to work at.

The offices of the two small French companies Pons and Huot are amazing. Each of the 15 people who work there has his or her own "dome" – a private work space. There is also a meeting room, a kitchen and restrooms, and lots of plants and trees everywhere.

Google Ireland has employees from 38 countries who speak 46 different languages. The atmosphere is very relaxed. When the weather is nice, employees have meetings outside on comfortable seats called beanbag chairs.

The office of Grupo Gallegos, an advertising company, was once a movie theater. It has a wonderful view of the Pacific Ocean. The offices are open-plan, and 360 white umbrellas hang from the ceiling. There is a basketball court where workers can play and relax during their breaks.

B **Scanning for detail** What do the following numbers refer to?

| 31 | 15 | 46 | 360 | 38 |

C **Comprehension**

1 Which office is special because of
   A its ceiling?
   B its employees' individual work space?
   C its positive environment?

2 In which office can employees
   A play basketball during their breaks?
   B sit on comfortable chairs in meetings?
   C choose where they work?

D **Now you** Which office do you like best? Why?

 I can understand a text about different offices.

A) Write the symbols next to the words (1–9).

+	a	@
A	-	–
.	3	b

1 at ....
2 uppercase ....
3 dot ....
4 hyphen ....
5 plus ....

6 number ....
7 lowercase ....
8 underscore ....
9 dash ....

B) Complete the email with the words in the box.

attached   Attachment   Best regards   Dear
From   Subject   Thank   To

1 .... : mayumi-suger@mailasia.com

2 .... : yorkschool@cloud.com

3 .... : Language course in England

4 .... : York School of English.pdf

5 .... Ms. Sato:

6 .... you for your email. Please find 7 .... details of our
English courses in York.

If you have any questions, please contact us.

8 .... ,
Robert White
Sales Assistant

C) Write the email Mayumi Sato wrote to York School in 6B. Use these phrases:

I saw an advertisement for York School . . . (where?)
I am interested in an English course for . . . (how long? when?)
I am learning English . . . (where?), *but I need more practice.*
Could you send me . . . (what? a brochure – details – price list – dates)

- If you don't know the name of the person you're
  writing to, begin: *Hello* or (formal) *Dear Sir or Madam.*

- End the email:
  Sincerely, (formal)
  Best regards, (less formal)
  Best, (informal)

I can write an email to ask for information.

TOEIC® practice

1 Listening

A **|10| Photographs** Listen. Then choose the sentence that best describes the photograph.

1 A ☐   B ☐   C ☐   D ☐   2 A ☐   B ☐   C ☐   D ☐

B **|11| Question-Response** Listen carefully. Choose the best response to the sentence you hear.

Example: When is your next holiday?
A ☑ In May.   B ☐ Last week.   C ☐ On Bali.

1 A ☐   B ☐   C ☐   3 A ☐   B ☐   C ☐
2 A ☐   B ☐   C ☐   4 A ☐   B ☐   C ☐

2 Speaking

A **Describe a picture** Choose one of the pictures in part 1A. Look at it for 30 seconds, then describe it in your own words.

B **Read a text aloud** You have 45 seconds to look at the text below. Then you have 45 seconds to read it aloud.

> Cintya Dewi is a web designer. She works in the information technology department of a big company in Jakarta. Cintya gets up at seven o'clock. She goes to work by car. It takes about an hour and a half. She gets to the office at nine-thirty. First she makes coffee, then she turns on her computer. She doesn't eat lunch with her colleagues. She usually has a sandwich at her desk. She spends the evenings with her two little children.

3 Reading

Incomplete sentences Choose the best word to complete each sentence.

1 .... was your flight?
- [ ] **A** What
- [ ] **B** Who
- [ ] **C** Why
- [ ] **D** How

2 Are you here .... business?
- [ ] **A** for
- [ ] **B** on
- [ ] **C** at
- [ ] **D** in

3 Shall I .... you a taxi?
- [ ] **A** ask
- [ ] **B** drive
- [ ] **C** call
- [ ] **D** bring

4 Hiroshi is a marketing ....
- [ ] **A** producer
- [ ] **B** manager
- [ ] **C** designer
- [ ] **D** developer

5 Cintya knows the .... in her department.
- [ ] **A** friends
- [ ] **B** family
- [ ] **C** company
- [ ] **D** colleagues

6 Nadia .... a uniform at work.
- [ ] **A** carries
- [ ] **B** trains
- [ ] **C** wears
- [ ] **D** knows

4 Writing

Write a sentence based on a picture Write ONE sentence based on each picture. You must use the two words or phrases that are given with the picture.

Example: never / Mondays
Possible answer: *Ken is never in his office on Mondays.*

1 beach / weekend

2 often / late

18

On the phone

1 Business situation
Can I take a message?

Singapore

Osaka

Bangkok

Hiroshi

A **12** Hiroshi Akimoto of GameZ is making phone calls. Listen to the three calls. Match the person with the information.

1 James Neo, Singapore Software Systems ....

2 Anocha Thongdee, ThaiWeb Designs ....

3 Greg Murray, GameZ ....

A Hiroshi leaves a message for him/her.

B Hiroshi speaks to him/her.

C Hiroshi will call back later.

B **12** Listen again. Check (✔) the expressions that you hear.

	Call 1	Call 2	Call 3
1 Can he call you back?	☐	☐	☐
2 Could you repeat it, please?	☐	☐	☐
3 Speaking.	☐	☐	☐
4 I'll put you through.	☐	☐	☐
5 Can I take a message?	☐	☐	☐
6 Can I leave a message?	☐	☐	☐
7 I'll call back later.	☐	☐	☐
8 How can I help you?	☐	☐	☐
9 He's talking on the other line.	☐	☐	☐
10 I'll give him the message as soon as possible.	☐	☐	☐

▷ ▪ to repeat ▪ to take a message ▪ to leave a message
▪ client ▪ to call back

I can understand telephone phrases.

2 | Grammar focus
Present simple and present continuous

A | 12 | Listen again and complete the sentences.

1 Mr. Neo .... on the other line **at the moment**.
2 They .... lunch.
3 Greg: I .... at the new designs **right now**.

B Complete the rule.

> The present continuous is formed with the verb to .... +
> the .... form of the verb.

C Write sentences for these pictures.

1 I *am having lunch.*
2 Kasem ....
3 Mai ....
4 The cat ....
5 We ....
6 The colleagues ....

D Work with a partner.

Student A: Go to Partner file 2.
Student B: Look at the activities below. Pretend you're doing these things:

brush your teeth	make a phone call	drink a cup of tea	play the piano	write an email

Try to guess what your partner is doing. Take turns asking and answering questions.

Think of other activities to show your partner.

Are you .... ing?

Yes, I'm .... ing.

No, I'm not .... ing.

E Look at these examples and complete the rule.

Present simple	Present continuous
Hiroshi usually **works** late,	but this evening he **isn't working** late because it's his wife's birthday.
Hiroshi and Greg often **have** lunch together.	Today they are **having** lunch in the cafeteria with a client.
Anocha **writes** emails every morning.	Right now she **is writing** an email to her boss.

We use the **present** .... to talk about things that are happening now.
We use the **present** .... to talk about things that often happen.

The "double *do*": the verb *to do* also needs *do* or *does* in a question.

What <u>do</u> you <u>do</u>?   *What <u>does</u> he <u>do</u>?*

F Put the verbs in the correct form of the present tense.

1 Greg *usually works* (usually / work) in London, but *this month he is working* (this month / work) in Osaka.

2 **A:** Can I speak to Mr. Young? I .... (call) about the new course.
   B: No, sorry, he .... (talk) to another student at the moment. Can you call back later?

3 **A:** Listen! ....
      (ring / your phone)?
   B: Yes. I ....
      (expect) a call from my parents.
      They ....
      (always / call) me on Sundays.

I HOPE YOU'RE PREPARING FOR THE CONFERENCE IN HAWAII.

YOU BET!

4 Mai .... (usually / leave) the office at five o'clock. Now it is five o'clock, but Mai .... (not leave) the office. She .... (stay) longer today.

5 .... (they / attend) the conference in Hawaii this week?

6 **A:** What .... (you / work) on at the moment?
   B: I .... (prepare) a presentation for the next lesson.

7 Christine is on a business trip in Osaka. She .... (enjoy) the trip. She .... (always / enjoy) her trips to Osaka.

Use short forms in conversation:

I am → I'm   *we are → we're*   *they are → they're*

▸ • right now • at the moment
   • to expect • to attend

I can talk about what people are doing now.

3 Listening and speaking
On the phone

A | 13 | One morning in the office there are six voicemail messages for Hiroshi Akimoto. His assistant writes down the messages, but she makes a mistake in each one. Listen to the messages and correct the mistakes.

1
Greg wants to meet for lunch at 1:30. Please let him know if it's OK.

2
Please call back James Neo from Singapore Software Systems this morning.

3
Takeshi wants to meet in his office after work. Please call back.

4
Ms. Klein wants to talk about her next trip to Osaka. She will call back.

5
Mr. Neo phoned again. His cell phone number is 010 65 8653 1827.

6
The Key Supply Company can't send the new equipment next month.

B Talking about ... cell phones

Step 1: What functions are important to you in a cell phone? Give each function a number from 5 (= very important) to 1 (= not important).

- ☐ battery life
- ☐ camera
- ☐ color
- ☐ games
- ☐ Internet
- ☐ music
- ☐ quality of display
- ☐ size
- ☐ streaming TV
- ☐ text messages

Step 2: Why are the functions important or not important? Make notes.

Step 3: Compare your list with a partner.

Which functions are most important / not important to you?

Why is it important / not important to you?

Step 4: Tell the class what you and your partner(s) have found out.

Mai and I think that . . . is very important because . . .

Gan and I prefer . . . to . . . because . . .

We never . . .

▷ ▪ equipment ▪ function ▪ battery

I can understand telephone messages and talk about cell phones.

Vocabulary focus

Focus 1: Spelling names and saying numbers

A 〔14〕 **Listen to people spelling their names. Choose which name you hear.**

1	☐ Rosita	☐ Rozite	☐ Rozita
2	☐ Jeony	☐ Yeonyi	☐ Yeone
3	☐ Shirley	☐ Shirlee	☐ Chirley
4	☐ Gerri	☐ Jirri	☐ Jerri

B 〔15〕 **It's not always easy to understand when people spell a name. So businesspeople all over the world often use the International Telephone Alphabet when they spell things on the phone. Listen to the alphabet.**

A for Alfa	**J** for Juliet	**S** for Sierra
B for Bravo	**K** for Kilo	**T** for Tango
C for Charlie	**L** for Lima	**U** for Uniform
D for Delta	**M** for Mike	**V** for Victor
E for Echo	**N** for November	**W** for Whiskey
F for Foxtrot	**O** for Oscar	**X** for X-ray
G for Golf	**P** for Papa	**Y** for Yankee
H for Hotel	**Q** for Quebec	**Z** for Zulu
I for India	**R** for Romeo	

C 〔16〕 **Listen to the people spelling their names and write them down.**

1 ....   4 ....
2 ....   5 ....
3 ....   6 ....

D **Work with a partner. Use the International Telephone Alphabet and spell:**

1 your own full name
2 a friend's full name
3 the name of a famous person

Your partner writes down the names for you to check. Then change roles.

1 ....
2 ....
3 ....

E **Look at this number:** +61 (0)3 1234567-21

Complete the sentences with these words:

extension number	area code	subscriber number	country code

+61 is the ....   (0)3 is the ....
1234567 is the ....   21 is the ....

Tell a partner.
1 What is the country code for your country? Do you know any other country codes?
2 What is the area code for your town? What other area codes do you know?

In telephone numbers 0 in American English is usually *zero*.

In British English it's *oh*.

I can spell names.

Vocabulary focus

Focus 2: Telephone language

F Remember the telephone phrases from 1B? Complete the sentences. There is one extra word.

back	call	help	leave	line	message	possible	repeat	speak	through

1 Could you .... that, please?
2 How can I .... you?
3 I'll put you ....
4 Can I .... a message?
5 He's talking on the other ....
6 Can he call you .... ?
7 I'll .... again later.
8 I'll give him the message as soon as ....
9 Can I take a .... ?

G Make a phone call with a partner. Follow the conversation plan.

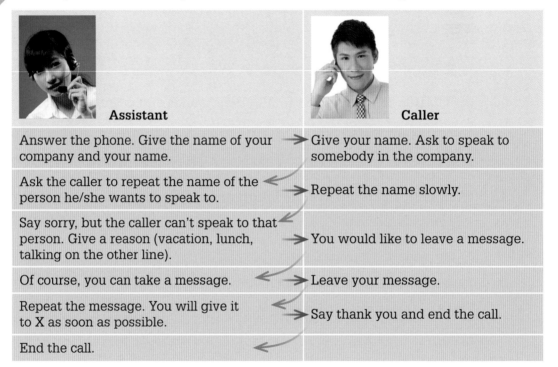

Assistant	**Caller**
Answer the phone. Give the name of your company and your name.	Give your name. Ask to speak to somebody in the company.
Ask the caller to repeat the name of the person he/she wants to speak to.	Repeat the name slowly.
Say sorry, but the caller can't speak to that person. Give a reason (vacation, lunch, talking on the other line).	You would like to leave a message.
Of course, you can take a message.	Leave your message.
Repeat the message. You will give it to X as soon as possible.	Say thank you and end the call.
End the call.	

H ▷ **Key words** Look at the words at the bottom of pages 19–22. Choose the best words to complete the sentences.

1 Could you .... your name, please?
2 Sorry, he's not here .... Can you .... later?
3 She isn't here .... Can I .... a .... ?
4 Kim always .... the office meetings.
5 Mai has a lot of technical .... in her room.
6 I can't use my phone because the .... is dead.
7 Kamin .... to pass his exams.
8 Hiroshi often has lunch with a ....

I can use telephone language.

Reading
The unbreakable cell phone

A **Before you read** Have you lost or broken your cell phone before? What happened? Tell a partner.

Asian Business **Online**
looks at a new development in the world of cell phones.

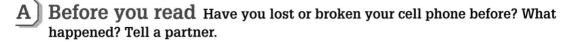

Samsung is developing a flexible smartphone that you can roll up like a piece of paper. This is possible thanks to a wonder material called "graphene."

Graphene is a very light but very strong material made from graphite – and graphite is something we all know – it's the gray stuff in our pencils!

Graphene was discovered in 2004. It's such an amazing material that the two scientists who discovered it got the Nobel Prize for Physics in 2010.

Smartphone users touch their screens hundreds of times a day, so the screens have to be very strong. And smartphones must also be light, so you don't notice them in your pocket. Graphene is much stronger and lighter than the material we are using at the moment to make smartphone screens. It's also much, much cheaper.

Samsung is not the only company that is working on projects with this attractive new material. Both Nokia and IBM are looking at different uses for graphene. So let the future begin!

B **Scanning for detail** Find out about graphene. Are the statements correct? If not, correct them.

1 It's the material we have in our pencils. ....
2 Samsung discovered it. ....
3 It was discovered in 2010. ....
4 It's attractive because it's light and flexible. ....
5 It's very strong but very expensive. ....
6 You can only use it for smartphone screens. ....

C **Comprehension**

1 What prize did the two scientists get and why?
2 Why do smartphone screens need to be very strong?

D **Now you** Work with a partner. Tell him/her:

• what kind of cell phone you have.
• something you don't like about your phone.
• which apps you use the most and why.
• if you would like a graphene phone and why (not).

I can understand a text about new smartphones.

Culture focus
Business cards in Asia

A Label the business card with the words in the box 1 to 7.

1 address	**5** logo
2 company name	**6** job title
3 email address	**7** phone number
4 first and last names	

GameZ

Hiroshi Akimoto
Marketing Manager

9 Shiromi, Chuo-ku
Osaka, 530-0047
Japan
Tel: 81 06 69462992
email: gamez@webmaster.konami.co.jp

Game Z

B Read the text and answer these questions.

1 In which countries do you present your card with both hands?
2 In which country do you present your card with one hand?
3 How is Korea different from other Asian countries?
4 How do you present a business card in your country?

Presenting a business card

In China, you should present your card before you ask for the other person's card. It's a good idea to have a Chinese translation on one side of your card. But make sure It's in the correct dialect, Mandarin or Cantonese. In China and in Japan, you should present the card with both hands. Bow or nod, and thank the person for meeting you. Never put the card away immediately, and never write on the card.

When you get a business card in Korea, nod your head to show respect and thank the person for meeting you. Korea is different from other Asian countries – you can put the card away immediately. Don't look at the card too long because this is impolite.

In India, businesspeople give each other their cards after the first handshake and greeting. Your card should show your academic degree. Give and take cards with your right hand – you should also do this in all Islamic countries.

I can read a text about business cards in Asia.

Buying and selling

1 Business situation
Helping customers

17 Listen to three conversations between a store clerk and his customers. Check the correct answer.

Conversation 1

1 The store has some .... thumb drives

- [ ] **A** 16 GB and 32 GB
- [ ] **B** 32 GB and 64 GB
- [ ] **C** 16 GB and 64 GB

2 The customer decides to buy a .... gigabyte thumb drive.

- [ ] **A** 16
- [ ] **B** 32
- [ ] **C** 64

Conversation 2

3 The customer wants to buy

- [ ] **A** a smartphone for his girlfriend.
- [ ] **B** a tablet for himself.
- [ ] **C** a tablet for his girlfriend.

4 The store

- [ ] **A** doesn't have any smartphones.
- [ ] **B** sells smartphones and tablets.
- [ ] **C** has some smartphones on sale.

Conversation 3

5 The customer needs

- [ ] **A** a TV for his dad.
- [ ] **B** a converter box.
- [ ] **C** some videos.

6 The customer

- [ ] **A** wants to pay less than $100.
- [ ] **B** buys the item and leaves the store.
- [ ] **C** asks to see some cheaper items.

▷ ▪ store clerk ▪ customer ▪ size
  ▪ on sale ▪ to connect

I can understand a conversation in a store.

Grammar focus
Focus 1: *some* and *any*

A 🔊 17 Listen to the conversations again and complete the sentences.

- **Conversation 1**
  Store clerk: Do you need .... help?
  Customer: Do you have .... thumb drives?
  Store clerk: We have .... 32 gigabyte drives
  Store clerk: No, sorry. We don't have .... bigger drives.

- **Conversation 2**
  Store clerk: We have .... great smartphones
  Customer: Do you have .... tablets with Wi-Fi?

- **Conversation 3**
  Store clerk: Do you have .... boxes that are
  not too expensive?
  Customer: We don't have .... cheap ones left

B Complete the rule for *some* and *any*.

> We use .... in positive statements.
> We use .... in negative statements.
> We use .... in questions.

> Sometimes you also hear questions with *some*:
>
> *Do you want some milk in your coffee?*

C Complete the sentences with *some* or *any*.

1 I need .... large thumb drives. I don't need .... small ones.
2 Do you have .... converter boxes?
3 There aren't .... cheap tablets left.
4 We have .... smartphones on sale, but we don't have .... tablets.
5 I don't have .... money left.
6 Do you have .... 64 gigabyte thumb drives?

D Work with a partner.

Student A: Go to Partner file 3.
Student B: Look at the pictures below of things you have and don't have in your office. Answer your partner's questions.

Yes, I have some books in my office. No, I don't have any coffee.

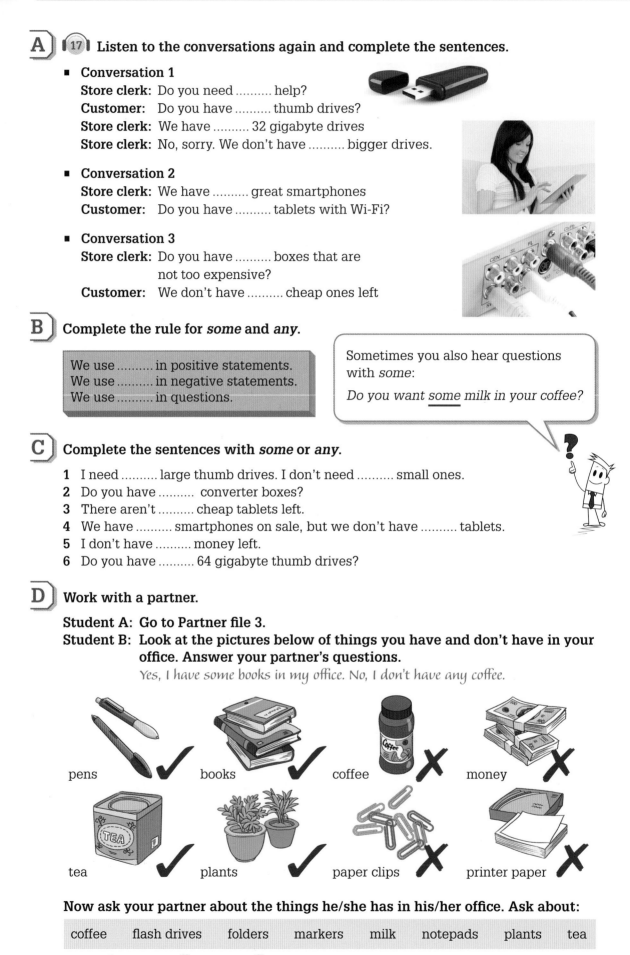

pens ✓   books ✓   coffee ✗   money ✗

tea ✓   plants ✓   paper clips ✗   printer paper ✗

Now ask your partner about the things he/she has in his/her office. Ask about:

coffee	flash drives	folders	markers	milk	notepads	plants	tea

Do you have any coffee in your office?

Grammar focus
Focus 2: *much* and *many*

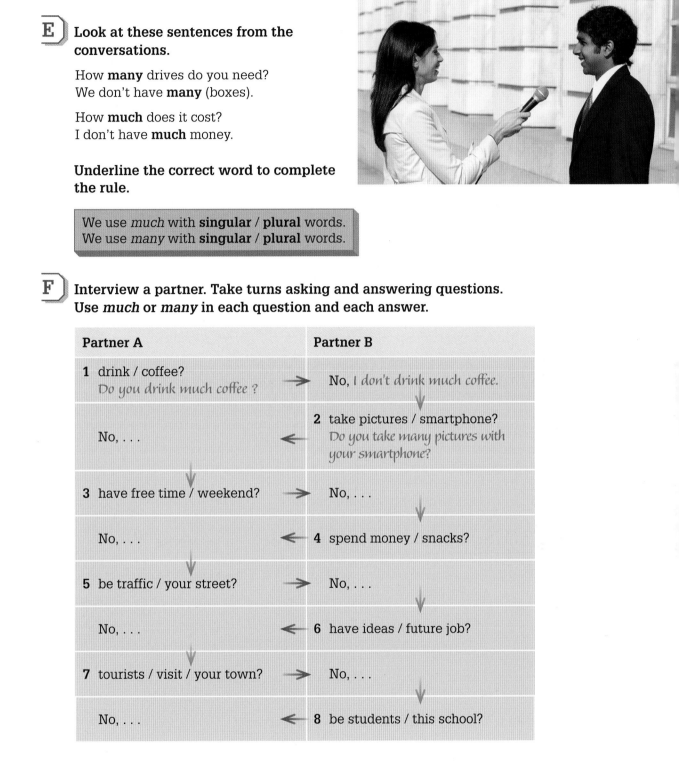

E Look at these sentences from the conversations.

How **many** drives do you need?
We don't have **many** (boxes).

How **much** does it cost?
I don't have **much** money.

Underline the correct word to complete the rule.

> We use *much* with **singular** / **plural** words.
> We use *many* with **singular** / **plural** words.

F Interview a partner. Take turns asking and answering questions.
Use *much* or *many* in each question and each answer.

Partner A	Partner B
1 drink / coffee? *Do you drink much coffee ?* →	No, *I don't drink much coffee.*
No, . . . ←	**2** take pictures / smartphone? *Do you take many pictures with your smartphone?*
3 have free time / weekend? →	No, . . .
No, . . .	← **4** spend money / snacks?
5 be traffic / your street? →	No, . . .
No, . . .	← **6** have ideas / future job?
7 tourists / visit / your town? →	No, . . .
No, . . .	← **8** be students / this school?

We can use *a lot of* in statements with singular and plural words:

How much coffee do you drink? – I drink *a lot of* coffee.

How many books does he have? He has *a lot of* books.

▷ ▪ gift ▪ (the) latest ▪ (none) left

> *I can* ask and answer questions with *some/any* and *much/many*.

Listening and speaking
Shopping habits

A Look at the pictures. How do you think Liu and Huan like to shop?

Liu

Huan

Liu likes . . .   *Huan prefers . . .*

B [18] Listen to Liu and Huan talking about their shopping habits. List . . .

1 three things that Liu and her friends do at the shopping mall.
2 three reasons why Liu doesn't like shopping online.
3 three reasons why Huan doesn't like shopping at a mall.
4 three things Huan says are better when you shop online.

C Listen to Liu and Huan again. Are the statements correct? If not, correct them.

1 Liu goes shopping with her sister.
2 Liu sometimes shops online.
3 Huan buys all his clothes online.
4 Huan likes to experiment with clothes.

D Talking about ... shopping: good and bad service

Step 1: Discuss in small groups. What do you like and dislike about the service in stores, online and offline? Think about:

choice of things	fast/late delivery	prices	product information
sold out	store hours	(un)helpful staff	

I like it when . . .   There are some things I really dislike . . .
If the store clerk can't . . . , I . . .

Step 2: Make a list of your group's likes and dislikes.

We like it when . . .	We dislike it when . . .
a store has a large choice of things.	store clerks can't give us any information.
....	....

Step 3: Tell the class what is on your list. Make a class list together.

▷ ▪ shopping mall ▪ to compare ▪ to try on
▪ can't afford ▪ brand ▪ choice

I can talk about shopping habits and service in stores.

Vocabulary focus

Focus 1: Giving directions

A (19) **Listen and mark your answers on the map.**

1 Where are the people standing?
2 Where are the restrooms?

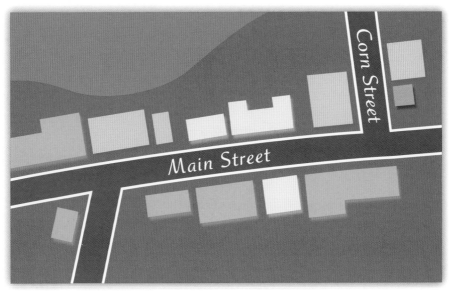

B (19) **Listen again and complete the sentences.**

1 Go .... down this street.
2 Turn .... onto Main Street.
3 Turn .... onto Corn Street.
4 The restrooms are on the right .... the sushi bar and .... the bookstore.

C (20) **Liu is telling her friend how to get to Alta Moda. Listen and find out where these places are on the floor plan of the shopping mall. Write the letter next to the place.**

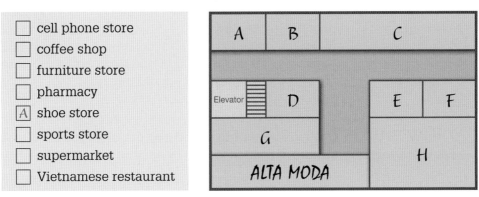

☐ cell phone store
☐ coffee shop
☐ furniture store
☐ pharmacy
A shoe store
☐ sports store
☐ supermarket
☐ Vietnamese restaurant

D **Work with a partner. Think of a place in your town (bus station, shopping mall, park, etc.), but don't tell your partner. Describe how to get there. Can your partner guess what place it is?**

When you leave this building, turn . . .
You are at . . . Go straight . . .

I can understand and give directions.

Vocabulary focus
Focus 2: Words that go together (2)

E Match the words 1 to 10 and A to J.

1	on	D	**A**	size
2	waste	....	**B**	breaks
3	right	....	**C**	online
4	compare	....	**D**	~~sale~~
5	electronic	....	**E**	time
6	take	....	**F**	shopper
7	shopping	....	**G**	drive
8	shop	....	**H**	mall
9	online	....	**I**	equipment
10	thumb	....	**J**	prices

F Complete the sentences. Use some of the word pairs from 4E.

Every Saturday Yui and her friend Hina go to the .... and spend the whole day there. They go from store to store so that they can .... and look for things that are .... – things that are a bit cheaper than usual. They always try on clothes and shoes to be sure that they are the .... They often .... for coffee or ice cream. Yui never goes shopping with her boyfriend. He prefers to .... He hates to .... in the shopping mall. He buys everything online from clothes to ....

G Which words go together? Check (✔) or cross (✘).

1	waste	✔	time	✔	paper	✔	money	✘	shops
2	expensive	☐	money	☐	clothes	☐	brand	☐	tablet
3	shopping	☐	online	☐	mall	☐	supermarket	☐	on Saturdays
4	busy	☐	person	☐	computer	☐	shopping mall	☐	street
5	try on	☐	shoes	☐	clothes	☐	thumb drive	☐	quality

H ▷ **Key words** Look at the words at the bottom of pages 27–30. Choose the best word to complete the sentences.

1 The .... wants to help the ....
2 Sorry, we don't have any 16 gigabyte drives ....
3 There are many different kinds of stores in a ....
4 Tablets are .... this week – only $300.
5 What .... are you looking for? – Nike.
6 It's easy to .... prices on the Internet.
7 Do you have the .... smartphone?
8 I .... a tablet. They're too expensive.

I can use words that go together.

Reading
Showrooming

A **Before you read** Look at the title of the article and the photo. What do you think the article will be about?

Asian Business **Online**
looks at "showrooming," a modern way of shopping.

Do you ever see something in a store, try it on, check the price online on your smartphone, find it is cheaper, and walk out of the store? Welcome to the world of "showrooming."

You are not the only person who does this, and it is becoming a major problem for store owners. Clothing stores, stores for electronic equipment, bookstores, and cosmetics stores are all losing business.

Amy Fu, 23, lives and shops in Singapore. She sometimes spends $200 in an afternoon, but not in the stores she visits. "I can go in and smell a perfume, and then find it online $20 cheaper," she says. "Sometimes when the staff are very helpful, I feel bad. But it's my money."

Online stores can offer cheaper prices because they don't have the costs of a building and staff. Some shoes and clothing stores in Australia ask for a fee when someone tries something on. The fee is taken off the bill when someone buys something.

Steve Richards, who has an English bookstore in Singapore, says: "We see customers in the corner with their cell phones. We know what they are doing, but we can't stop them. We can only hope they feel uncomfortable when they know we are watching them."

Of course, online stores such as Amazon want "real" stores to survive so that people can see, touch, and try on products. So perhaps one day online stores will have real showrooms, but only to look and try on – not to buy. All buying and selling will be online.

B **Scanning for detail** Find the missing information.

1 Showrooming is a big problem for .... (who?).
2 Amy Fu sometimes spends .... (how much?) in an afternoon.
3 Amy Fu sometimes buys .... (what?) online.
4 Online stores can offer cheaper prices because .... (why?).
5 Steve Richards hopes customers feel uncomfortable .... (when/what?).
6 Online stores want "real" shops to survive so that .... (why?).
7 Perhaps one day online stores will have .... (what?).

C **Vocabulary in context** Scan the text and find words that mean:

1 leave
2 very big
3 less expensive
4 people who work in a store
5 money for a service
6 not die

D **Now you**

1 Do you shop online? Why (not)?
2 Do you prefer online shopping to shopping in a store? Why (not)?

I can understand a text about the future of shopping.

Business writing
An inquiry

You are the owner of a toy store. One day you see this advertisement. You are interested in the RobotBird and other toys for your store.

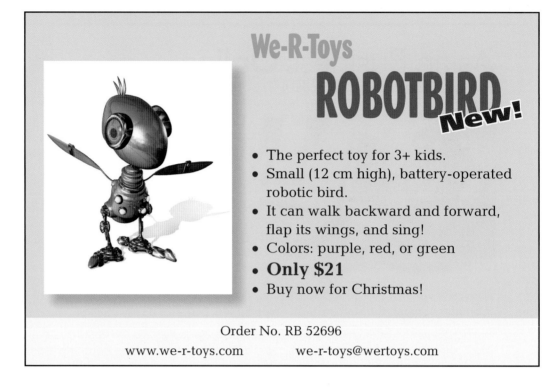

We-R-Toys

ROBOTBIRD New!

- The perfect toy for 3+ kids.
- Small (12 cm high), battery-operated robotic bird.
- It can walk backward and forward, flap its wings, and sing!
- Colors: purple, red, or green
- **Only $21**
- Buy now for Christmas!

Order No. RB 52696

www.we-r-toys.com   we-r-toys@wertoys.com

Write an email to We-R-Toys. Remember the rules for emails from Unit 2.

Say who you are.
  I am the owner of . . .

Say why you are writing.
  I would like more information about . . .

Talk about quantities and colors.
  For my store I need . . .

Ask about special prices.
  . . . for larger quantities?

Say you are interested in other toys and ask for a catalog.
  I am also . . . Would you please . . . ?

Close the email.

Subject: . . .

Dear . . . :

I saw your advertisement for . . .

The *subject line* should be short, so people can read quickly what the email is about.

I can write an email asking for product information.

TOEIC® practice

1 Listening

A 🔊 21 **Photographs** Listen. Then choose the sentence that best describes the photograph.

1 A ☐ B ☐ C ☐ D ☐   2 A ☐ B ☐ C ☐ D ☐

B 🔊 22 **Conversations** Listen and answer the questions.

Conversation 1

1 What does the green top cost?

☐ **A** $15
☐ **B** $50
☐ **C** $13
☐ **D** $30

2 Which statement is correct?

☐ **A** The woman doesn't like green.
☐ **B** The woman can't afford to buy anything.
☐ **C** The T-shirts cost the same as the tops.
☐ **D** The woman's size is medium.

3 What does the woman buy?

☐ **A** a green top
☐ **B** a blue top
☐ **C** a green T-shirt
☐ **D** a blue T-shirt

Conversation 2

1 Who is the woman calling?

☐ **A** a supermarket
☐ **B** her hairdresser
☐ **C** her dentist
☐ **D** a car wash

2 Why is the woman calling?

☐ **A** to make an appointment
☐ **B** to order a product
☐ **C** to check her calendar
☐ **D** to say hello to Carlo

3 When will the woman see Carlo?

☐ **A** on Thursday at three o'clock
☐ **B** on Friday at three o'clock
☐ **C** on Thursday at four o'clock
☐ **D** on Friday at four o'clock

2 Speaking

Describe a picture Choose one of the pictures in 1A. Look at it for 30 seconds, then describe it in your own words.

3 Reading

Text completion Read the email. Choose the best word to complete each sentence.

Dear Suzie,

Thanks for your email. You want to know about a typical day **1** .... work.

- ☐ **A** for
- ☐ **B** on
- ☐ **C** to
- ☐ **D** at

Well, we **2** .... very early. I **3** .... to the office at about nine-thirty.

- ☐ **A** don't start
- ☐ **B** not start
- ☐ **C** start not
- ☐ **D** are not starting

- ☐ **A** go usually
- ☐ **B** usually go
- ☐ **C** am usually going
- ☐ **D** usually do go

I read and write emails. I also answer the phone and **4** .... messages.

- ☐ **A** leave
- ☐ **B** want
- ☐ **C** take
- ☐ **D** say

I usually leave the office at six o'clock. That's a typical day.

Best wishes,
Max

4 Writing

Respond to a written request Ask for at least TWO more pieces of information.

From: Suzie Tseng
To: Max Bird
Subject: A typical day
Sent: July 9, 4:15 PM

Hi Max,

Thanks for your email. You asked me to tell you about a typical Saturday. On Saturdays I always go to the shopping mall with my girlfriends. I love shopping in the mall.

What about you? Do you like shopping? Could you tell me something about your shopping habits?

Best wishes,
Suzie

What are you doing tomorrow?

1 Business situation
Making an appointment

 John Santos works for Greencheck Software, an American company in Manila. He is Dr. Mark Little's assistant. John is in the office one morning when the telephone rings. Listen to the conversation and find six mistakes in the text below.

John: John Santos, Greencheck Software. How can I help you?

Mr. Parks: Can I speak to Dr. Little, please? My name's David Parks. Dr. Little and I were in New York at a conference last week. This week I'm in Manila. Dr. Little is expecting my call.

John: I'm sorry, Mr. Parks. He's in a meeting right now, but he wants me to make an appointment with you.

Mr. Parks: Fine. Can you make a suggestion?

John: Let me see, mmm, today's Monday. Is later today possible?

Mr. Parks: No, sorry. I'm having lunch with a client at noon, and later today I'm attending a workshop. What about tomorrow?

John: I'm sorry. Dr. Little has a lot of appointments on Wednesday. Let's look at Thursday.

Mr. Parks: No, no. On Thursday I'm meeting some friends. What about the day after?

John: Friday is no problem. What's better for you, the morning or the afternoon?

Mr. Parks: The morning is better for me.

John: Well, why don't you come late morning, Mr. Parks? Then you can have coffee with Dr. Little.

Mr. Parks: That's a good idea. Shall we say eleven-thirty?

John: Fine. Friday at eleven-thirty. Thank you for your call. Goodbye.

> ▪ appointment ▪ suggestion
> ▪ workshop ▪ noon

I can understand a conversation about making appointments.

Grammar focus
Present continuous for future plans

A Look at these sentences from the conversation. Are they about the *past*, *present*, or *future*? Write the time next to each sentence.

He's in a meeting right now. ....
Later today I'm attending a workshop. ....
On Thursday I'm meeting some clients. ....

Complete the rule.

We can use the present continuous in two ways:
1 to talk about ....
2 to talk about ....

B Write *P* for the sentences that talk about the present and *F* for the sentences that talk about the future.

1 What are you doing tomorrow? ....
2 John is busy. He's writing emails. ....
3 Where are you spending your next vacation? ....
4 Why are you wearing a raincoat? ....
5 Look, the train is arriving. ....
6 We're having a meeting later today. ....

C Use the words to ask questions about the future.

1 what time / Mr. Parks / arrive / on Friday?
   What time is Mr. Parks arriving on Friday?
2 who / Mr. Parks / meet / for lunch tomorrow?
3 you / go / out / tonight?
4 when / you / see / Huan / again?
5 where / John / going / on vacation next year?
6 Lan and Diu / play / tennis / next Sunday morning?

We also use the present continuous just before you do something in the future:

The meeting is in five minutes.
– Yes, I'm coming.

D Work with a partner. Ask about future plans. Take turns answering.

	this evening?
	tomorrow?
What are you doing	this weekend?
	next Monday?
	when you finish your studies?

I'm meeting . . . We're . . .
I'm going to . . .

Work with a partner. Dr. Little has plans for a business trip next week.

Student A: Go to Partner file 4.

Student B: You have Dr. Little's agenda for next week, but some of the information is missing. Ask Student A for the missing information and answer your partner's questions. Use these verbs:

arrive (2x)	do	~~leave~~	meet	take

B: *What time is Dr. Little leaving on Monday?*
A: *He's . . .*

July

15 Monday	– Flight CZ 7976 – .... *(what time?)* Manila – London
16 Tuesday	– .... *(what time?)* arrive London – two nights in King's Hotel
17 Wednesday	– 10:30 AM meet .... *(who?)*
18 Thursday	– 12:30 PM lunch with Marion Smith – .... *(when?)* train to Liverpool – Mersey Hotel
19 Friday	– 10 AM .... *(what?)* – Flight CZ 7934 – 6 PM Liverpool – London – Manila
20 Saturday	– .... *(when?)* arrive Manila

▷ ▪ business trip ▪ agenda
  ▪ to worry (about) ▪ to take a train

I can discuss future plans.

3

Listening and speaking
Making plans and suggestions

A [24] Lien Hu works for a music company in Hong Kong. She and her team are discussing plans for the production of a new album by the boy band SuperAsia. Listen and complete the sentences.

Plans for this week

Tomorrow   Lien is giving *a presentation.*

Thursday 10 AM Lien, Huan, and Ken are having a meeting about the band's

....

Friday 2 PM   Lien is meeting ....

Plans for next week

Tuesday 5 PM
The band is coming to the office to
....

Tuesday 7 PM
The band, their agent, and
Lien's team are having
....
at ....
called Amigo.

Wednesday 8 AM
The band is recording in
....

Friday
Ken ....
with the designer, and she
.... some cover
designs with her.

B [24] Listen again. Which of these phrases for making suggestions do you hear?

☐ *Let's . . .*
☐ *Would it be possible . . . ?*
☐ *Perhaps you should . . .*
☐ *What about . . . ing?*

☐ *Do you think we could . . . ?*
☐ *You could . . .*
☐ *Why don't you . . . ?*
☐ *Should we . . . ?*

C Work in groups of three. Make suggestions for these things.

Your friend wants to . . .
1 make a lot of money.
2 start his/her own company.
3 make friends in other countries.

4 go somewhere interesting on vacation.
5 get fit.
6 improve his/her English.

▷ ▪ agent ▪ necessary ▪ to sign ▪ contract
   ▪ promotion campaign ▪ to improve

I can understand a discussion about plans and make suggestions.

4 Vocabulary focus
Focus 1: Days, months, dates

A [25] **Listen and repeat the days of the week.**

Monday   Tuesday   Wednesday   Thursday
Friday   Saturday   Sunday

B [26] **Listen and repeat the months of the year.**

January	April	July	October
February	May	August	November
March	June	September	December

C [27] **Listen and repeat the dates.**

July 2, 2010   August 3, 1996   December 25, 1945   February 11, 1966

We write: *April 1, 2015.*   We say: *April first two thousand and fifteen.*

1/4 = January 4 (American English); April 1 (British English)

D [28] **Listen to the conversations and fill in the days, months, and dates.**

1 **A:** Does the product come onto the market on .... ?
   B: No, on ....
2 **A:** Are you flying to Tokyo on .... ?
   B: No, I'm flying on ...., and the meeting is on ....
3 **A:** Your birthday is in ...., isn't it?
   B: No, it's on ....
4 **A:** When is the next workshop?
   B: It's on ....

E **Fill in the missing prepositions.**

in + year/month	**on** + day	**at** + a festival/time
in 2015, in September	*on Monday, on my birthday*	*at Christmas, at four o'clock*

1 **A:** When were you born?
   B: .... 1996.
2 **A:** Do you ever give a party?
   B: Yes, every year .... my birthday.
3 **A:** When is your birthday?
   B: .... May.
4 **A:** What time do you usually get up?
   B: .... seven-thirty.
5 **A:** When do you usually go shopping?
   B: .... Saturdays.
6 **A:** When do you give gifts?
   B: .... Christmas.

F **Work with a partner. Ask and answer the questions in 4E.**

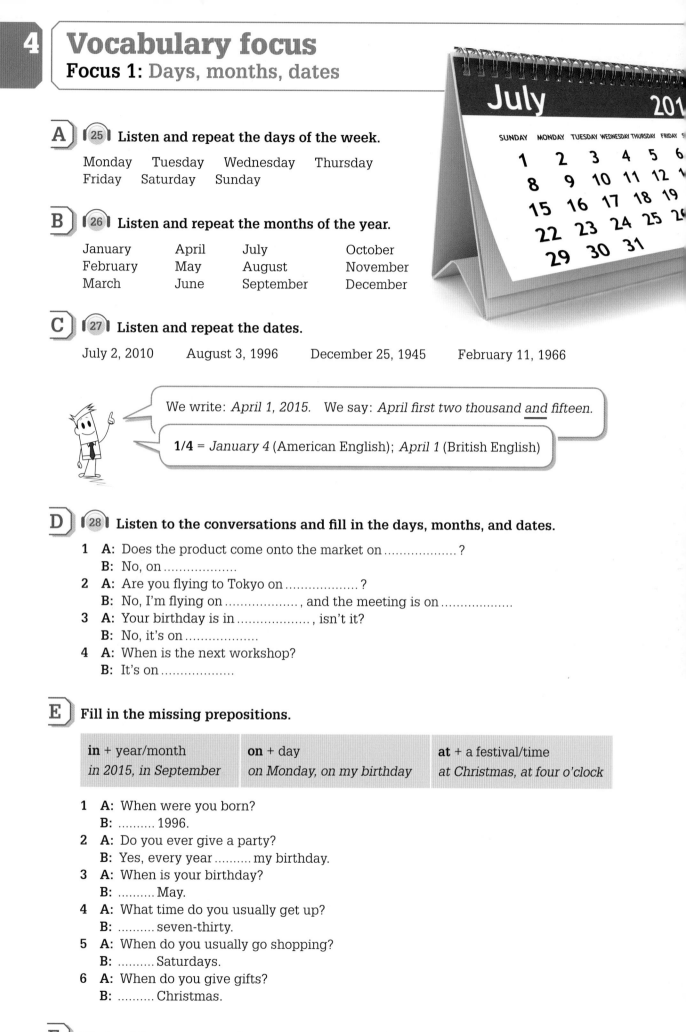

4

Vocabulary focus
Focus 2: Telling the time

G **29** **Listen and number the times in the order that you hear them.**

1 *It's twenty-five to eight in the morning.*

05:30 ☐	07:35 ☐1	08:20 ☐	11:15 ☐	12:00 ☐
14:45 ☐	15:30 ☐	18:40 ☐	20:45 ☐	19:00 ☐

> **5:10 AM**: We say *5:10 AM* **or** *ten past five in the morning.*
> **5:50 PM**: We say *5:50 PM* **or** *ten to six in the afternoon.*

H **Work with a partner. Ask and answer the questions.**

What time do you usually . . .
1 go to bed on weekdays and on the weekend?
2 get up on weekdays and on the weekend?
3 leave home in the morning?
4 have lunch?

I **Look at the time map. Greenwich Mean Time (GMT) is the time in London.**

1 Make sentences about the cities on the map.
When it's noon in London, it's three o'clock in the afternoon in Riyadh.
2 What time is it now where you are? What time is it now in the cities on the map?

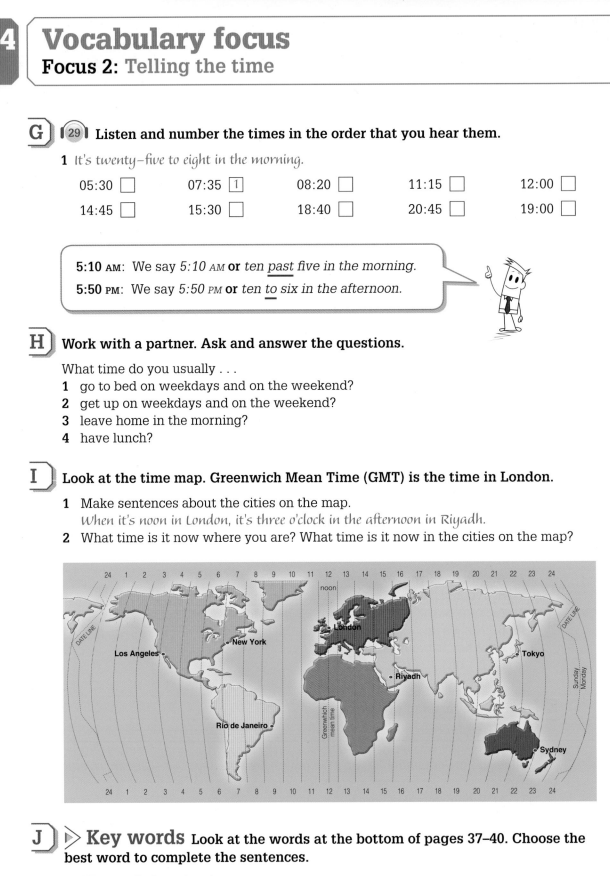

J ▷ **Key words** Look at the words at the bottom of pages 37–40. Choose the best word to complete the sentences.

1 We usually have lunch at ....
2 You don't need to help me. It's not ....
3 I sometimes .... my exams.
4 I always write my appointments in my ....
5 Dr. Little is going on a .... next week.
6 The band's .... is signing the .... tomorrow.
7 What is the best way to .... my English?
8 Can I make a .... ?

> *I can* talk about times and dates.

A) Before you read Work with a partner. Compare travel by train and by air. What is better? What is not so good?

Asian Business **Online**
looks at Chinese high-speed trains and plans for the future.

(A) Passengers may soon travel by train from London to Beijing in just 48 hours on trains that travel almost as fast as airplanes.

(B) China is planning to build a high-speed rail network to India and Europe within the next 10 years, with trains that can go at over 250 mph.

(C) The network would carry passengers from London to Beijing and then to Singapore. It would also go to India and Pakistan. Passengers could get on a train in London and step off in Beijing, over 5,000 miles away, in just two days. They could go on to Singapore, 6,750 miles away, and be there three days after leaving London.

(D) Another project plans to have trains that go south to connect Vietnam, Thailand, Myanmar, and Malaysia. Construction for the South East Asian line has already begun in the southern province of Yunnan, and Myanmar is planning to build its link. At present the only rail line that links China to South East Asia is a very old line built by the French in Vietnam a hundred years ago.

(E) China itself already has the greatest length of high-speed rail in the world. It aims to connect up all of its major cities with high-speed lines. It is planning to build 19,000 miles of new railways in the next five years. China has the world's fastest train, the Harmony Express. It runs between the cities of Wuhan and Guangzhou and has a top speed of nearly 250 mph.

B) The main idea Make paragrah headings with the words in 1 to 6. Then match them with paragraphs A to E.

1 mph / 250 / over   *Over 250 mph* .... B
2 airplanes / as / fast / as ....
3 train / the / fastest / world's ....
4 two / miles / in / 5,000 / days ....
5 East / Asia / South / linking ....

C) Comprehension

1 How long is the journey on a high-speed train
 – from London to Beijing?
 – from London to Singapore?
2 How far is it
 – from London to Beijing?
 – from Beijing to Singapore?
3 The article talks about three different projects. What are they?
4 Describe the present rail link between China and South East Asia.
5 Give three facts about the world's fastest train: its name, its speed, its route.

D) Now you

1 Are there fast trains in your country?
2 Do you enjoy traveling by train? Why (not)?

I can *understand the main idea of a text about future plans.*

A ❘30❘ Millie Dresser from Australia is an expert on international communication. She is talking about different communication styles. Listen and check (✔) the correct box.

Which country?	Australia	China	Germany
1 People have no problem with the word "no."	✔		
2 It is important to watch a person's body language.			
3 Businesspeople are formal.			
4 It is usual to use first names with business partners.			
5 It is OK to interrupt people in meetings.			
6 Businesspeople don't feel comfortable with small talk.			
7 People like working in teams.			

B Who do you think said it? Write *A* for an Australian, *C* for a Chinese, or *G* for a German. Sometimes more than one answer is possible.

1 Well, no, I'm sorry, but I can't show you the new software today.
   I'm busy. ....
2 Good morning, Chief Accountant Kam. ....
3 Jim, my business partner, is coming for a meeting today. ....
4 No, no, no . . . that's wrong! I don't agree! ....
5 I really like working in teams. ....
6 We don't have time for small talk. Let's get down to business. ....
7 Excuse me, but I must interrupt you there. ....

C Which communication style is the style in your country? Give some examples.

In my country when we . . .
We aren't like . . . We always . . .

I can understand different communication styles.

Out and about

1 ## Business situation
Customer service in a hotel

A 〔31〕 **Lucy Chen is a reservations clerk at the Plaza Hotel in Sydney. Listen to the conversations and complete the sentences.**

Conversation 1: The caller wants to ....
Conversation 2: The caller informs the hotel that ....

B 〔31〕 **Listen again. Match the sentence parts.**

1	I have a reservation	....	**A**	a single room on those dates.
2	I would like to	....	**B**	at twelve-thirty at the latest.
3	I'm sorry, we don't have	....	**C**	twenty-four hours a day.
4	Can you confirm	....	**D**	of your late arrival.
5	We have someone at reception	....	**E**	the reservation by email?
6	Let me	....	**F**	for three nights.
7	I expect to arrive	....	**G**	stay for two more nights.
8	I can inform my colleagues	....	**H**	just check that.

C **Work with a partner.**

Student A: Go to Partner file 5.
Student B: Prepare a conversation with your partner. Then read it to the class.

– You have a reservation at the Plaza Hotel for a double room for three nights, May 21–24.
– You want to stay an extra night.

– Call the hotel to ask if that is possible.
– Ask about the price for the extra night.
– Accept the offer.
– Ask the hotel to confirm the reservation.

A: *The Plaza Hotel. How can I help you?*
B: *Hello. My name is . . . I have a reservation for . . .*

 ▪ to reserve ▪ reservation ▪ single room
▪ double room ▪ comfortable ▪ to confirm

I can change a hotel reservation on the phone.

A | **[31]** **Listen again to Lucy Chen's conversations. Complete the sentences.**

The double room is .... and .... than a single room, but of course, it's ....

I can give you one of our .... rooms at a special price.

It's one of our .... rooms.

Complete the rules.

> **Comparative:** Add .... to a short adjective.
> We use the word .... with a long adjective.
> **Superlative:** Add .... to a short adjective.
> We use the word .... with a long adjective.

Marriage is for better or for worse.

> These are different:
>
> | | Comparative | Superlative |
> |---|---|---|
> | good | better | best |
> | bad | worse | worst |

B | **Read what they said and complete the rule.**

Lucy Chen: The double room is bigger
and more comfortable **than** a single room.
Mr Wijaya: He'll be there earlier **than** me.

> We use the word .... when we compare people or things.

C | **Akio and his sister Naoko are from Japan. Make sentences and compare the two of them.**

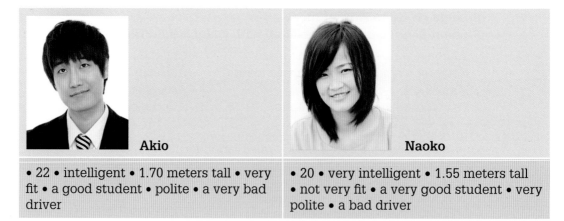

Akio	Naoko
• 22 • intelligent • 1.70 meters tall • very fit • a good student • polite • a very bad driver	• 20 • very intelligent • 1.55 meters tall • not very fit • a very good student • very polite • a bad driver

Akio is older than Naoko.
Naoko is more intelligent than Akio.

Look at the chart. Are the sentences true or false? Correct the false sentences.

	Indonesia	Singapore	Thailand
Size	about 2 million sq km	about 700 sq km	about 500,000 sq km
Population	240 million	5.3 million	70 million
People per sq km	130	7,800	140
Average age	30 years	33 years	35 years
Rent for new apartment in the capital	Jakarta: $700 per month	Singapore: $1,800 per month	Bangkok: $800 per month

1 Thailand is bigger than Indonesia.
   False. Thailand is smaller than Indonesia. / Indonesia is bigger than Thailand.
2 The population of Indonesia is the smallest.
3 Thailand is more crowded than Indonesia.
4 The population of Singapore is younger than the population of Indonesia.
5 An apartment in Bangkok is cheaper than an apartment in Jakarta.
6 The most expensive apartment is in Jakarta.
7 The population of Thailand is the youngest.
8 The most crowded country is Singapore.

E Write sentences with *not as . . . as.*

1 rents – high – Bangkok – Singapore
   *Rents **aren't as** high in Bangkok **as** in Singapore.*

2 rents – high – Jakarta – Bangkok
   ....

3 average age – low – Thailand – Indonesia
   ....

4 the population – large – Singapore – Thailand
   ....

5 the number of people per square kilometer – high – Thailand – Singapore
   ....

6 big – Indonesia – Thailand
   ....

My friend's apartment isn't as small as mine.

▷ ▪ population ▪ average ▪ cheap
  ▪ expensive ▪ crowded

I can compare people, places, and things.

3 Listening and speaking
Giving advice

A [32] Sinittra Tongsuk is talking to her Australian colleague, Tony. Tony is traveling on a long-haul flight for the first time next week. He's a bit nervous and asks Sinittra for advice. Listen to the conversation and check (✔) the advice you hear.

		Do	Don't
1	Go to bed as late as possible the night before.	☐	☐
2	Have only light meals before the flight.	☐	☐
3	Leave home early.	☐	☐
4	Wear your business clothes.	☐	☐
5	Take only light clothes with you on the plane.	☐	☐
6	Drink a couple of beers before the flight.	☐	☐
7	Stay in your seat during the flight.	☐	☐
8	Play computer games.	☐	☐

B Talking about ... traveling

Step 1: Read the questions and think about your answers.

Questions about travel habits	Ideas		Reasons
Where do you like to spend your vacations?	• the beach • the mountains • a city • the countryside		• exciting • quiet • adventure • relaxing
What kind of vacation do you like?	• adventure vacation • backpacking • beach vacation • language course	• coach trip • camping • skiing	• play sports • meet people • improve my English • have fun
How do you like to travel?	• by bus • by car • by coach • by train	• by plane • by bicycle • on foot	• fast • cheap • comfortable
What sort of place do you like to stay?	• hotel • guest house	• campsite • friends	• exciting • interesting

Step 2: In small groups, ask and answer the questions about your travel habits.

Step 3: Make notes for your group. Which are the most popular things? Why?

Step 4: Tell the class the results of your group survey.

> *For our group the most popular place to spend a vacation is . . . because . . .*
> *The most popular kind of vacation is . . . because . . .*
> *We like to travel by/on . . . because . . .*
> *Most of us like to stay in/on/at/with . . . because . . .*

▷ ▪ advice ▪ long-haul
▪ nervous ▪ to enjoy

I can talk about vacations and ways to travel.

Vocabulary focus

Focus 1: Traveling

A Read what these people say about their vacations. What kinds of vacations are they talking about? Look at exercise 3B.

1 "We walked about 20 kilometers every day."
2 "We spent every day just relaxing in the sun."
3 "It was difficult to put up the tent when it was windy."
4 "I decided to do English because it's easier than French."
5 "It wasn't very good. There wasn't enough snow."
6 "The bus was big and comfortable, but seven days on the road was a bit too much."

B You often do these things when you travel. Match the verbs (1–10) with the words and phrases (A–J).

1	change	....	**A**	a ticket
2	make	....	**B**	at the check-in desk
3	take	....	**C**	a car
4	buy	....	**D**	some shopping
5	rent	....	**E**	a taxi to the airport
6	line up	....	**F**	trains
7	do	....	**G**	business class
8	fly	....	**H**	a reservation
9	board	....	**I**	your passport
10	show	....	**J**	at gate 5

C Make two teams and do the travel quiz. The first team with each right answer gets a point.

1 What is the difference between a one-way ticket and a round-trip ticket?
2 A plane *lands* at the end of its journey. What does it do at the beginning?
3 What is the word for the money you pay to travel on a plane, train, or bus?
4 This tells us what time trains or planes arrive and leave.
5 Where do you usually stand when you're waiting for a train?
6 What is the name of the document with your seat number and gate number on it?
7 What do you call the bags you carry onto the plane?

I can use different words to talk about traveling.

D Look at the phrases we use to describe pictures.

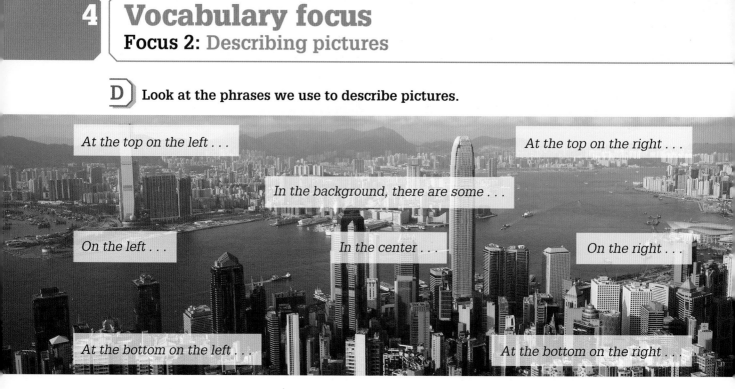

At the top on the left . . .

At the top on the right . . .

In the background, there are some . . .

On the left . . .

In the center . . .

On the right . . .

At the bottom on the left . . .

At the bottom on the right . . .

Work with a partner.

Student A: Go to Partner file 6.
Student B:
1 Look at pictures A and B. Which picture is your partner describing?

A

B

2 Describe this picture to your partner.

E ▷ **Key words** Look at the words at the bottom of pages 45–48. Choose the best word to complete the sentences.

1 I'd like to make a .... for a .... for my wife and me.
2 We will .... your reservation by email.
3 The .... age of the .... of Singapore is 33 years.
4 Let me give you some ....
5 The opposite of cheap is ....
6 It's Tony's first .... flight, and he's ....
7 Hundreds of people were in the shopping mall. It was very ....
8 **A:** Did you .... the flight?
   B: Not much. It isn't very .... in economy class.

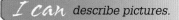

I can describe pictures.

5

Reading
The Richmond Hotel, Jakarta

A) Before you read What facilities does a business traveler need in a hotel?
Skim the article to see which facilities it talks about.

☐ Internet   ☐ swimming pool   ☐ laundry service

☐ satellite TV   ☐ bar   ☐ other

Asian Business **Online**
looks at readers' comments on last month's hotel review.

A "I agree with everything you wrote in your review of the Richmond Hotel. The central location is ideal for business travelers. The hotel restaurant is first class. Unfortunately, when I stayed there, the Wi-Fi signal in my room was not good, and this was a great disadvantage."

B "A very nice hotel with a fantastic staff and excellent facilities, including large, bright conference rooms. The gym and the rooftop pool are great to relax in after a day's work. As you said in your review, the rooms are large and comfortable with high-speed internet connections and satellite TV. I travel a lot, but staying at the Richmond is always special."

C "I don't agree with your review at all! I spent two nights at the Richmond on my last business trip to Jakarta. My room was small, and the bathroom was not very clean. The air conditioning was noisy and the breakfast poor. I used the gym, but it was very small and crowded. I don't recommend this hotel. The only good thing about it is the location."

D "The Richmond is a large hotel with an unattractive lobby. But the staff are very friendly and the service excellent. I met clients for lunch and dinner in the Executive Lounge on the top floor, and we all agreed that the food was delicious. The laundry service is expensive but good. Not the best hotel I know, but it's good value for the money."

B) Scanning for detail Which of comments A, B, C or D talk about . . .

1 the food in the hotel. ....   4 the gym. ....

2 the location of the hotel. ....   5 the size of the rooms. ....

3 the hotel staff. ....   6 telecommunications. ....

C) What do you think? How many stars did the writers give the hotel? Why?

	★	★★	★★★	★★★★	★★★★★
A	☐	☐	☐	☐	☐
B	☐	☐	☐	☐	☐
C	☐	☐	☐	☐	☐
D	☐	☐	☐	☐	☐

I can understand comments on a hotel.

A Read Lucy's confirmation of Jenny Bond's reservation in 1A.
Underline the words and phrases that fit best.

In American English, write: *Dear Ms. Bond:*

In British English, write: *Dear Ms Bond,*

From: plazahotel@plaza.com
To: jennybond@google.com
Subject: Confirmation of your reservation

Dear **1** . . . (Ms. Bond / Jenny):

I **2** . . . (like / would like) to confirm your reservation at the Plaza Hotel **3** . . . (as follows / like this):

Room: double room
Number of nights: 5
Date: March 19–24
Total price: $600

If you **4** . . . (have any questions / want anything), please contact us.

5 . . . (Please enjoy / We hope you enjoy) your stay with us at the Plaza Hotel.

6 . . . (Best / Sincerely),
Lucy Chen

Reservations Clerk
The Plaza Hotel
Tel. (612) 9250 3608
Fax (612) 9250 3609

B [33] You are the reservations clerk at the Richmond Hotel. Listen to the
conversation and make notes. Then write a confirmation. Use the language in
6A. Don't forget the subject line.

From: BusinessHotel@Richmond.com
To: emma.sari@msn.com
Subject:

I can write a confirmation email.

TOEIC® practice

1 Listening

A) [34] **Photographs** Listen. Then choose the sentence that best describes the photograph.

1 A ☐ B ☐ C ☐ D ☐

2 A ☐ B ☐ C ☐ D ☐

B) [35] **Talks** You will hear a talk by a tour guide. Choose the best answer to each question.

1 What will the tour group do first?
- ☐ **A** Go for lunch.
- ☐ **B** Take a walk in the park.
- ☐ **C** Visit Ground Zero.
- ☐ **D** Listen to a talk on the World Trade Center.

2 How much time will the group have to walk in the park?
- ☐ **A** one hour
- ☐ **B** one-and-a-half hours
- ☐ **C** until 3 PM
- ☐ **D** no limit

3 In the late afternoon the tour guide will
- ☐ **A** take all the tourists to the zoo.
- ☐ **B** take some of the tourists to the zoo.
- ☐ **C** listen to Beatles songs with the tourists.
- ☐ **D** go to the Dakota building.

2 Speaking

[36] **Respond to questions** Answer three questions. For each question, you must answer immediately after the beep.

Imagine you work at the reception desk of a hotel in the center of your town or city. A hotel guest is asking you for information about your town or city.

1 What are the hours of the stores here?
2 What are the best places to visit on foot?
3 Are there any good restaurants nearby?

3 Reading

Reading comprehension Read the text and choose the best answer to each question.

Hotel Bellavista is on the banks of the Arno, which flows through Italy's main wine region into the Ligurian Sea. Only twenty minutes by car from the city center, the hotel is a small, friendly, family business. We have four single rooms and three doubles. The hotel has its own quiet garden where you can relax and enjoy the wine we produce ourselves. Our restaurant offers excellent meals cooked in the traditional Italian way. Enjoy our weekend special price: two nights for two people in a double luxury room with breakfast and dinner and our house wines for just €400. Make your reservation now.

1 Where is the hotel?

- [ ] **A** on a river
- [ ] **B** on a lake
- [ ] **C** in the city center
- [ ] **D** by the sea

2 The hotel has

- [ ] **A** seven rooms but no garden.
- [ ] **B** a garden but no restaurant.
- [ ] **C** four rooms and a restaurant.
- [ ] **D** a garden and a restaurant.

3 The hotel is

- [ ] **A** a luxury hotel.
- [ ] **B** a small, family hotel.
- [ ] **C** a traditional hotel.
- [ ] **D** an excellent hotel.

4 The special price of €400

- [ ] **A** is for bed and breakfast only.
- [ ] **B** is the price per person.
- [ ] **C** includes a room, meals, and wine.
- [ ] **D** is for any day except Saturday and Sunday.

4 Writing

Write a sentence based on a picture. Write ONE sentence based on each picture. You must use the two words or phrases that are given with the picture.

Example: learn / computer
Possible answer:
The children are learning to use a computer.

1 always / credit card

2 text message / airport

Tell me about your company

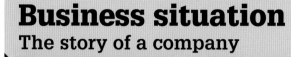

1 Business situation
The story of a company

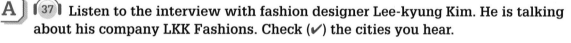

A **37** Listen to the interview with fashion designer Lee-kyung Kim. He is talking about his company LKK Fashions. Check (✔) the cities you hear.

1 ☐ Busan   4 ☐ Paris

2 ☐ London   5 ☐ Seoul

3 ☐ New York   6 ☐ Sydney

B **37** Listen to the interview again. Are the statements true or false? Correct the false statements.

	True	False
1 Lee-kyung Kim was born in 1989.		
2 He studied at a university in Seoul.		
3 He went to France in 2006.		
4 In France, he got the idea for his own company.		
5 He didn't want to stay in France.		
6 He worked for a fashion company in Busan.		
7 He didn't like his job in Busan.		
8 Lee-kyung started LKK Fashions when he was only 26 years old.		

▷ ▪ fashion designer ▪ to study ▪ experience
   ▪ success ▪ award

I can understand somebody talking about a company.

Grammar focus

Focus 1: Past simple – regular verbs

A 🔊 **37** **Listen to the interview with Lee-kyung Kim again. The verbs in brackets ( ) are *regular* verbs. Use them in the past tense to complete the sentences.**

1 Lee-kyung .... (return) to Korea at the beginning of 2009.
2 He .... (work) in Busan.
3 He .... (design) costumes for movies.
4 He .... (not want) to work for a large company any longer.
5 Lee-kyung, when .... you .... (decide) to specialize in men's fashion?
6 He .... (not expect) to win the Fashion Award.

B **Look at the statements and questions in 1B and 2A. Complete the rule.**

We use the past simple to talk about ....
For regular verbs we add .... to the verb.
We use .... in questions and .... in negatives.

We say:

I *didn't work*. NOT *I didn't ~~worked~~*.   *Did you work*? NOT *Did you ~~worked~~*?

C **On weekdays, Lee-kyung does the same things at work. Sundays are different. Yesterday was Sunday. What did Lee-kyung do? What didn't he do? Work with a partner. Ask and answer questions.**

1 walk to his studio

2 stay in bed late

3 talk to colleagues

4 open his mail

5 play tennis

6 watch a DVD

7 welcome a client

8 visit friends

9 listen to music

10 look at new designs

1 **A:** *Did he walk to his studio?*
  B: *No, he didn't walk to his studio.*

2 **A:** *Did he stay in bed late?*
  B: *Yes, he stayed in bed late.*

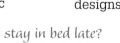

D **Work with a partner. Ask about last Sunday. Use questions from 2C.**

Grammar focus

Focus 2: Past simple – irregular verbs

E The verbs in brackets ( ) are *irregular* verbs. Use them in the past tense to complete the sentences. Look at the table of irregular verbs on page 95 to help you.

1 After he .... (leave) university, Lee-kyung .... (go) to France.
2 He .... (get) the idea for his own company when he .... (be) in France, but he .... (not have) enough money.
3 Lee-kyung, why .... you .... (leave) France?
4 The New Man fashion show .... (win) an award.

Note the past tense of the verb *to be*:

He was good at his job.   *When were you in Seoul?*

She wasn't the CEO*.   *They weren't in the office.*

* Chief Executive Officer

F Last Monday, Lee-kyung was in his studio. But on Tuesday he was on a business trip. What did Lee-kyung do on Monday? What didn't he do on Tuesday?

When he is in his studio, Lee-kyung . . .	Last Monday, Lee-kyung . . .	Last Tuesday, Lee-kyung . . .
1 sees his colleagues.	*saw his colleagues.*	*didn't see his colleagues.*
2 meets clients.	....	....
3 makes drawings.	....	....
4 has lunch with his assistant.	....	....
5 writes emails.	....	....

G Work with a partner. Ask questions and make a time line about your partner's life.

When were you born?   *What did you . . . ?*   *Where did you . . . ?*
Where were you . . . ?   *Who did you . . . ?*

be born	start school	live from . . . to	learn	meet

▷ ▪ costumes ▪ to specialize
   ▪ to win ▪ drawing

I can talk about things in the past.

Listening and speaking
Successful Asian companies

A 〔38〕 Listen to people talking about successful Asian companies and complete the table. It's not necessary to understand every word.

Company	Lenovo	HYUNDAI	OLAM	Asian Paints
Product	computer hardware			
Started		1967 in Seoul, South Korea		
Headquarters in . . .			Singapore	
Employees				5,000
Active in . . . countries				
Revenue (US$)				1.9 billion

B 〔38〕 Listen again and complete the sentences.

1 The Han-card was Lenovo's first successful ....
2 Lenovo's .... are in North Carolina.
3 The Hyundai Motor Company is the world's .... automobile producer.
4 The Hyundai Motor Company first sold cars in .... (country?) in 1986.
5 Olam International has over 12,000 .... worldwide.
6 Today, Olam deals with 20 different products from many different ....
7 .... (who?) started the Asian Paints company.
8 By 1967, Asian Paints was India's .... paint company.

C) **Talking about ...**) successful companies

Step 1: In small groups, decide on a company you want to talk about. (Or you can invent a company.)

Step 2: Research the company on the Internet. Make a chart like the one in 3A and note down the information.

Step 3: In your group, prepare a presentation.
We would like to talk about . . .
It's a company that produces/sells/ makes . . . (product)
It started in . . . (year) in . . . (place).
Today, the company is / company's headquarters are in . . .
It has . . . employees in . . . countries and has revenue of . . .

Step 4: Tell the class about the company.

▷ ▪ revenue ▪ headquarters ▪ employee
▪ vehicles ▪ worldwide

I can research and present information about a company.

4 Vocabulary focus
Focus 1: Countries and nationalities

A Work with a partner. Ask and answer questions. Match the companies and the nationalities.

Company	
1 Honda	F
2 L'Oreal	....
3 Samsung	....
4 BMW	....
5 Ikea	....
6 Zara	....
7 Red Bull	....
8 Shell	....
9 Tesco	....
10 The Tata Group	....

	Nationality	Country
A	Indian	India
B	German	Germany
C	Austrian	Austria
D	Dutch	The Netherlands
E	Korean	South Korea
F	~~Japanese~~	~~Japan~~
G	British	Britain
H	French	France
I	Swedish	Sweden
J	Spanish	Spain

A: *Is Honda Japanese?*
B: *Yes, it is. The company comes from Japan. Is L'Oreal . . . ?*
A: *No, I think it's . . . The company comes from . . .*

B Complete the sentences.

1 John lived in Korea for ten years, so he speaks perfect *Korean*.
2 Lee-kyung worked in .... for a long time, so his French is really good.
3 Cintya lived in Sweden for a few months, so she speaks a bit of ....
4 Noon went on vacation to .... last year, but she doesn't speak any German.
5 Hiroshi comes from .... , and he teaches Japanese.
6 Tony's wife is from Spain, and they speak .... together.
7 Mike visited some clients in .... , but he couldn't speak to them in Dutch.
8 Liu worked in Britain for six months, and there she learned ....

The names of languages are usually the same as the nationality:

He's Thai. He speaks Thai.

She's speaking Japanese, so she must be Japanese.

He speaks French – but he's Chinese, not French.

C Make two teams and have a competition. The first team to give a correct answer to a question below gets a point. The team with the most points wins.

Can you name . . .

1 an American coffee house?
2 a German drink?
3 an American automobile company?
4 a Swedish fashion company?
5 a Korean singer?
6 an American credit card company?
7 a French car?
8 a Japanese video game company?
9 a British actor?
10 a Chinese actress?

I can talk about countries and nationalities.

D Look at these sentences and complete the rule about *make* and *do*.

What did you **do** after you left university?
On weekdays, Lee-kyung **does** the same things at work.
Lee-kyung **makes** drawings.
Lee-kyung **made** a lot of money.

> We usually use .... as general verb or for an activity.
> We use .... when there is a product at the end.

E Complete the sentences with the correct form of *make* or *do*.

1

Lin – teacher

A: What .... you .... after school every day, Lin?
B: I .... the shopping for my family.

2

Jenna and Anna – secretaries

A: .... you .... tea or coffee, Jenna?
B: I .... tea. Would you like some?

3

Huang – cameraman

A: What .... you .... with that camera, Huang?
B: I .... a movie.

4

Kang – marketing manager

A: What .... you .... , Kang?
B: Right now I'm .... nothing.

F Work with a partner. Ask and answer questions about the people in 4E. Use *do* to talk about their jobs.

What does Lin do? — *She's a teacher.*

G ▷ **Key words** Look at the words at the bottom of pages 55–58. Choose the best words to complete the sentences.

1 Lee-kyung .... fashion because he wanted to be a ....
2 Lee-kyung's fashion show was a great ....
3 Lee-kyung got a lot of .... when he worked for the film company.
4 Today, Lee-kyung .... in men's fashion.
5 Lee-kyung hopes to .... another award.
6 Hyundai's .... are in Seoul.
7 The company's .... is about US$2 billion a year.
8 It's a big company and it has 5,000 ....

> *I can* ask and answer questions with make and do.

A **Before you read** Look at the picture and title of the article. What do you think the article is about? Tell a partner. Then skim the article and check your ideas.

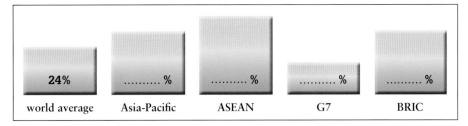

Asian Business **Online**
looks at women in senior management.

A new report shows that there are more women at the highest level of senior management than ever before. Globally, the percentage of women in any senior management position has risen from 20 percent a few years ago to 24 percent.

China leads. Over half of all senior management jobs are held by women, and as a region, Asia-Pacific is ahead of the rest of the world with 29 percent of all managers female. Within the Asia-Pacific region, ASEAN leads with 36 percent.

In the G7 countries – the US, the UK, France, Germany, Italy, Canada, and Japan – the figures are much lower, with just 21 percent of senior management jobs in the hands of women. The figure for the BRIC (Brazil, Russia, India, and China) economies is 28 percent.

One of the top jobs in senior management is the Chief Executive Officer (CEO). Only 14 percent of the world's CEOs are women. But in Thailand, an amazing 49 percent are women – the highest number in any country.

The reasons why Asia is above average are not clear. Are Asian women more ambitious than women in other countries? Do they fight harder to reach the top?

B **Scanning for detail** Fill in the missing figures for women in senior management.

24%	.... %	.... %	.... %	.... %
world average	Asia-Pacific	ASEAN	G7	BRIC

C **Comprehension** Read the article and choose the best answer.

1 A few years ago, women had .... of senior jobs globally.
  A one-quarter　**B** one-third　**C** one-fifth

2 The country with the most women in senior management jobs is ....
  A China.　**B** Thailand.　**C** the US.

3 .... of Thailand's CEOs are women.
  A 14 percent　**B** About half　**C** Most

4 The reason why the figure for women is so high in Asia is ....
  A because they are ambitious.　**B** because they fight harder.　**C** not known.

D **Now you** Why do you think Asia has above average figures?

I can understand a text about women in top jobs.

Culture focus
Conversation taboos

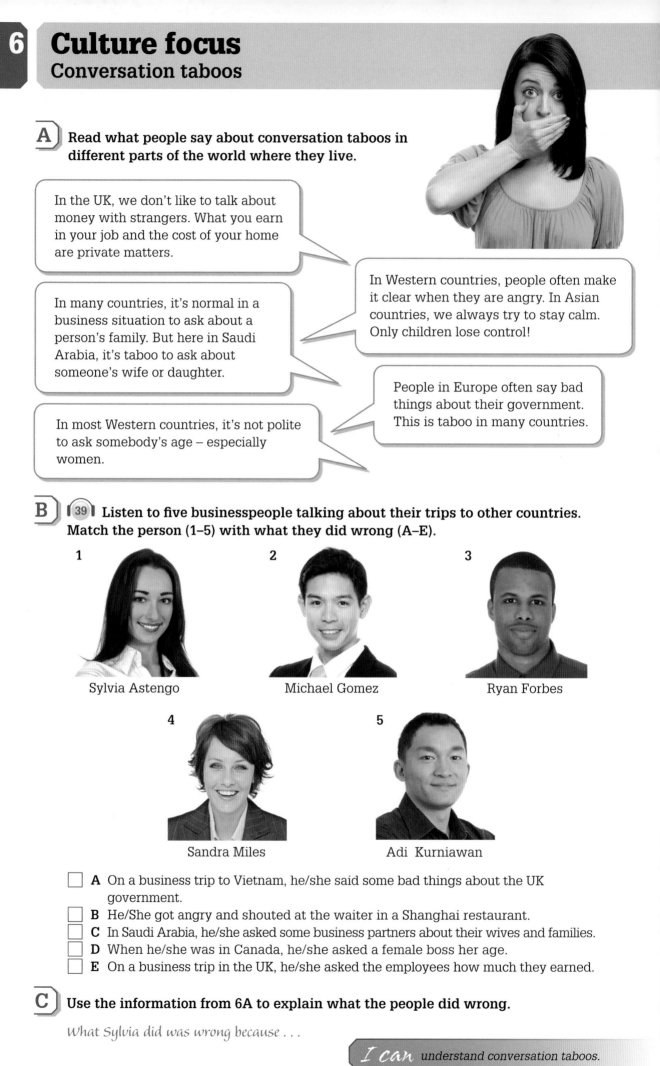

A Read what people say about conversation taboos in different parts of the world where they live.

> In the UK, we don't like to talk about money with strangers. What you earn in your job and the cost of your home are private matters.

> In Western countries, people often make it clear when they are angry. In Asian countries, we always try to stay calm. Only children lose control!

> In many countries, it's normal in a business situation to ask about a person's family. But here in Saudi Arabia, it's taboo to ask about someone's wife or daughter.

> People in Europe often say bad things about their government. This is taboo in many countries.

> In most Western countries, it's not polite to ask somebody's age – especially women.

B ❙39❙ Listen to five businesspeople talking about their trips to other countries. Match the person (1–5) with what they did wrong (A–E).

1 Sylvia Astengo

2 Michael Gomez

3 Ryan Forbes

4 Sandra Miles

5 Adi Kurniawan

☐ **A** On a business trip to Vietnam, he/she said some bad things about the UK government.

☐ **B** He/She got angry and shouted at the waiter in a Shanghai restaurant.

☐ **C** In Saudi Arabia, he/she asked some business partners about their wives and families.

☐ **D** When he/she was in Canada, he/she asked a female boss her age.

☐ **E** On a business trip in the UK, he/she asked the employees how much they earned.

C Use the information from 6A to explain what the people did wrong.

What Sylvia did was wrong because . . .

I can understand conversation taboos.

Let's eat out

1 Business situation
Entertaining in the business world

A [40] Amy Anderson works for a textile company in Singapore. Her British business partner, Marc Simpson, is in Singapore this week. Listen to the conversations. Who says what? Write *A* for Amy, *M* for Marc, or *R* for the man in the restaurant.

1 You mustn't leave Singapore before we have a chance to meet. ....
2 Yes, we must meet for lunch. ....
3 Everyone says that it's great and we have to try it. ....
4 I can't come tomorrow . . . I can come on Wednesday. ....
5 We can meet here, at my office. ....
6 Can I reserve a table for two? ....
7 You don't need to reserve a table for lunch. ....
8 You have to make a reservation if you want to come in the evening. ....
9 I don't speak it, but I can understand quite a lot. ....
10 I mustn't be late. ....

B [40] Listen to conversation 1 again and answer the question.

Where and when will Amy and Marc meet?

C [40] Listen to conversation 3 again and answer the questions.

1 What does Amy want to eat and drink?
2 What does Marc want to eat and drink?

▷ ▪ to invite ▪ invitation
▪ menu ▪ to suit

I can understand an invitation and a conversation in a restaurant.

2 Grammar focus
Focus 1: Modal verbs

A 🔊40 **Listen to the conversations again and complete the sentences.**

- **Conversation 1**
  Marc: We .... meet for lunch.

- **Conversation 2**
  Man: You .... reserve a table.
  Man: You .... make a reservation if you want to come in the evening.

- **Conversation 3**
  Marc: I don't speak it, but I .... understand quite a lot.
  Marc: I .... be late.

B **Talk about the road signs. Use the words below each sign.**

When you see this sign, you . . .

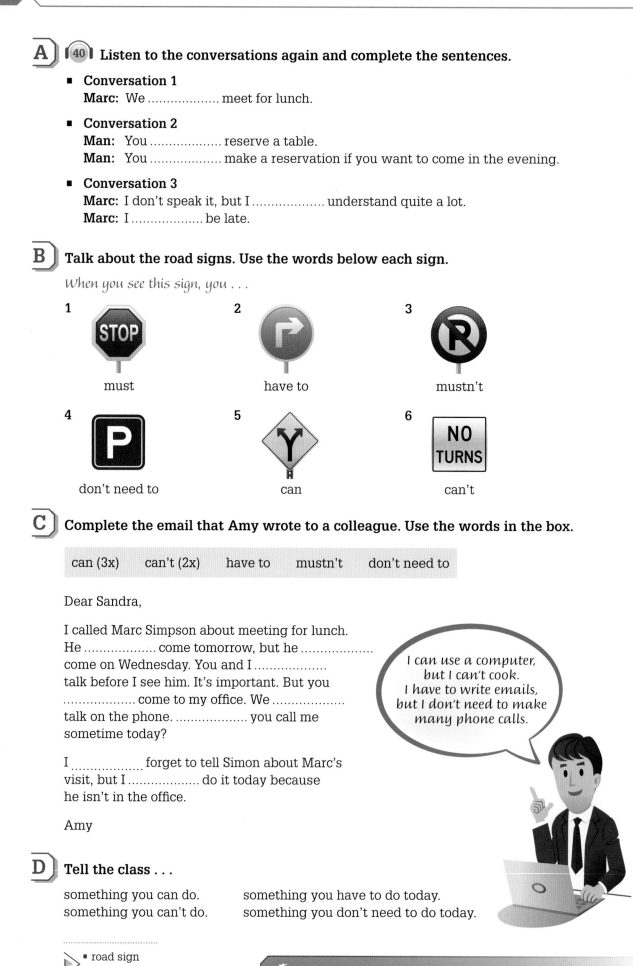

1	2	3
must	have to	mustn't
4	5	6
don't need to	can	can't

C **Complete the email that Amy wrote to a colleague. Use the words in the box.**

can (3x)	can't (2x)	have to	mustn't	don't need to

Dear Sandra,

I called Marc Simpson about meeting for lunch.
He .... come tomorrow, but he ....
come on Wednesday. You and I ....
talk before I see him. It's important. But you
.... come to my office. We ....
talk on the phone. .... you call me
sometime today?

I .... forget to tell Simon about Marc's
visit, but I .... do it today because
he isn't in the office.

Amy

> *I can use a computer,
> but I can't cook.
> I have to write emails,
> but I don't need to make
> many phone calls.*

D **Tell the class . . .**

something you can do.   something you have to do today.
something you can't do.   something you don't need to do today.

▷ • road sign

I can use the modal verbs can, must, have to, need to.

Grammar focus

Focus 2: Countable and uncountable nouns

E Look at the table and complete the rule below.

Countable nouns	Uncountable nouns
one, **a(n)** apple, banana, carrot, egg, melon, sandwich **two**, **three**, **four** apples, bananas, carrots, eggs, melons, sandwiches	bread, fish, fruit, meat, pasta, tea, water

We can count some words, for example .... and ....
We can't count other words, for example .... and ....

F Look at the sentences and underline the correct word in the rule below.

Amy: Pasta with salmon sounds good.
Marc: Mineral water is fine.

The verb after an uncountable noun is in the **singular / plural**.

G Are these words countable or uncountable? Add *a*, *an*, or *X* (= nothing).

1	*a*	tomato	**6**	....	sugar
2	*X*	milk	**7**	....	butter
3	....	orange	**8**	....	pineapple
4	....	rice	**9**	....	onion
5	....	strawberry	**10**	....	cheese

If we want to say a quantity with uncountable nouns, we say:

some meat, a kilo of pasta, two liters of water, three cups of tea.

H Correct the mistakes. One sentence is correct.

1 Can I have one bread, please?
2 Cook the pastas for ten minutes.
3 I would like one kilo of meats.
4 I ate ten strawberries and some grapes.
5 Use a liter water to cook the rice.
6 Do you want some butters on your bread?

I Make phrases with words from the two boxes.

a bottle of water

~~bottle~~	bowl	cup	piece	box	glass
eggs	meat	wine	~~water~~	rice	coffee

I can use countable and uncountable nouns.

A) **[41]** Tony Marshall is in Bangkok. He's having a quick lunch with his business partner, Chermarn Arak. Listen and put the sentences below in the order you hear them.

A What do you recommend? ....
B We can have something sweet for dessert. ....
C That sounds good. ....
D Can you explain it to me? ....
E Food courts are really popular here in Bangkok. 1
F What's that over there? ....
G What would you like to eat? ....
H That's a bit too spicy for me. ....

B) **[41]** Listen to the conversation again. Check (✔) the foods that you hear.

✔ bean sprouts	☐ egg	☐ pineapple	☐ seafood
☐ beef	☐ mango	☐ pork	☐ shrimp
☐ chicken	☐ noodles	☐ rice	☐ tofu
☐ coconut	☐ peanuts	☐ sauce	☐ vegetables

C) Work with a partner. You're in a food court in your country with a guest from abroad. Have the conversation and then change roles.

Student A	Student B
Ask Student B for his/her choice. *What would you . . . ?*	Ask Student B to recommend something. *What do you . . . ?*
Recommend a dish. *They have really good . . .*	Ask Student A to explain. *I don't know what that is. Can you . . . ?*
Explain the dish. *It's . . . with . . . You can have it with . . .*	Ask about dessert. *What can we . . . ?*
Suggest a dessert and describe it. *We can have . . . That's . . . / It's made of . . . / It comes with . . .*	

DeSSert with double S for Sweet Stuff.

A deSert is a dry place with lots of sand.

▷ • to recommend • dish • spicy
• dessert • delicious • diet

I can talk about a restaurant menu.

Vocabulary focus

4

Focus 1: Food and drink

A The names of the things in the pictures are wrong. Correct them and then make four lists with the things under these headings:
Fruit, Vegetables, Drinks, Fast food.

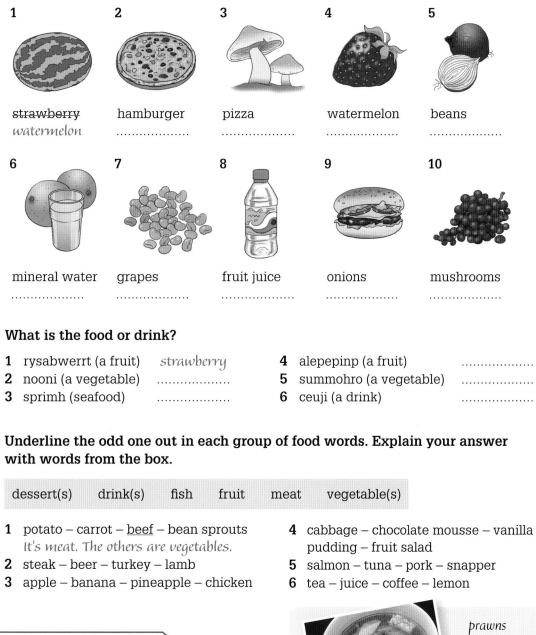

1
~~strawberry~~
watermelon

2
hamburger
....

3
pizza
....

4
watermelon
....

5
beans
....

6
mineral water
....

7
grapes
....

8
fruit juice
....

9
onions
....

10
mushrooms
....

B What is the food or drink?

1 rysabwerrt (a fruit)   *strawberry*
2 nooni (a vegetable)   ....
3 sprimh (seafood)   ....
4 alepepinp (a fruit)   ....
5 summohro (a vegetable)   ....
6 ceuji (a drink)   ....

C Underline the odd one out in each group of food words. Explain your answer with words from the box.

| dessert(s) | drink(s) | fish | fruit | meat | vegetable(s) |

1 potato – carrot – <u>beef</u> – bean sprouts
It's meat. The others are vegetables.
2 steak – beer – turkey – lamb
3 apple – banana – pineapple – chicken

4 cabbage – chocolate mousse – vanilla pudding – fruit salad
5 salmon – tuna – pork – snapper
6 tea – juice – coffee – lemon

D **Talking about ...** a favorite dish

Step 1: Think about your favorite dish. What do you need to make it? Use a dictionary to help you.

prawns
fish
mushrooms
lime
chilli . . .

Step 2: Work with a partner. Ask and answer questions about your dish. Ask . . .
– the name of the dish.
– what is in it.
– how often your partner eats it.
– where your partner usually eats it.

I can talk about food, drinks, and my favorite dish.

E Look at the conversation between Amy and Marc from 1A.

Amy: I'd like to invite you to lunch. . . . What about tomorrow?
Marc: Thanks for the invitation, Amy. . . . I'm afraid I can't come tomorrow.
Wednesday is better for me. I can come on Wednesday.

1 Which phrase does Amy use to invite Marc?
2 Which phrase does Amy use to suggest a time?
3 Which phrases does Marc use to
   A say thank you.   **B** say no.   **C** say yes.

F The sentences in the two conversations below are mixed up. Put them in the correct order.

A formal invitation	An informal invitation
☐ Eight is fine. I'm looking forward to it.	☐ Let's say seven-thirty in the hotel bar.
☐ That's very kind of you. I'd like that very much.	☐ I don't know what your plans are, Amy, but would you like to join us for a drink later on?
☐ If you have no plans for this evening, Mr. Simpson, I'd like to invite you to have dinner with us.	☐ Great. I'll be there at seven-thirty.
☐ Good. Shall I pick you up at your hotel at about eight?	☐ I'd love to. What time?

G Work with a partner. Take turns inviting each other to . . .

- visit our factory.
- come and meet our new CEO.
- look at our new offices.
- try the cheesecake in this café.
- come to our New Year's celebration.

Your partner can say yes or no. If it's no, suggest another time.

H ▷ **Key words** Look at the words at the bottom of pages 63–66. Choose the best words to complete the sentences.

1 No dessert for me, thanks. I'm on a ....
2 I can .... the chicken. It's very good.
3 What a .... meal!
4 Are there any Thai .... on the ....?
5 **A:** What does it say on that ....?
   B: It says "No parking."
6 Which day would .... you best?
7 This curry is too hot and .... for me.
8 Thank you for the .... to lunch.

I can invite somebody and say yes or no to an invitation.

Reading
Special requests on MJets

A **Before you read** What kind of people fly in private jets? Scan the article to see if your ideas are in the text.

Asian Business **Online**
looks at Asia's leading private jet service.

- Employees of MJets Ltd. were surprised when a Hollywood celebrity asked them for fried insects for her son on a private flight out of Bangkok.

- A famous beauty queen wanted to enjoy a special Szechuan-style soup in her executive jet. Unfortunately, she told the MJets staff of her wish only 10 minutes before departure.

- An Indonesian tycoon wanted grilled tapioca in syrup, a dessert from the cassava plant that has almost disappeared from Bangkok.

These are examples of the unusual requests from the rich and famous who travel in private planes. The Hollywood star's son, the beauty queen, and the Indonesian billionaire all got what they wanted, thanks to the excellent staff at MJets, Asia's leading private jet service.

MJets' customers are billionaires, VIPs, and rich business executives who fly around the world in private jets and spend a lot of money. MJets' services are expensive and individual. An Indian billionaire's wife asked MJets to organize an Indian meal for nine passengers on a flight one evening. "The food came in two trucks and cost $13,000," one employee remembers.

Most of the time, MJets knows what its customers will ask for. People from the Middle East like mangos and longans, so MJets carries lots of them when they fly to the United Arab Emirates. For flights to India they carry fresh Thai coconuts. Thai dishes such as green curry chicken and *som tam* (spicy papaya salad) are the most popular meals for foreign guests on flights out of Bangkok. It seems that *som tam* tastes even better at 10,000 meters!

B **The main idea** Which sentence gives the main idea of the text?

1 Rich people are different.
2 MJets' services are personal but very expensive.
3 MJets flies people from Bangkok all over the world.

C **Scanning for detail** Find the information.

1 Who requested
  – dinner for nine?
  – a special soup?
  – a snack for her son?
  – an unusual dessert?

2 What do MJets' planes carry when they fly to
  – the United Arab Emirates?
  – India?

D **Vocabulary in context** Find these words in the text.

1 someone who is famous, especially in show business ....
2 a rich and powerful businessperson ....
3 very, very good ....
4 a person on a high level in a company ....
5 the opposite of cheap ....
6 a large vehicle used to transport things ....
7 a noun from "to fly" ....

I can understand a text about a private jet service.

A Read the emails. Complete them with these phrases:

> I can reserve a table   I would like to join you   is fine with me
> I'm afraid   no other day is possible   that suits you
> I would like to   sounds good   Tuesday is not a good day for me

---

Dear Mr. Schmidt:

.... invite you and your colleague, Ms. Adams, to dinner after your visit to our company next week. Our Sales Manager, Mr. Choi, hopes to be there, too.

There is a very nice sushi bar restaurant across from your hotel in Tehran Road. .... for Tuesday evening at 8 PM.

Please let me know this week if .... I hope you can join us.

Best wishes,
Minsum Lee

Dear Ms. Lee:

Thank you very much for your invitation. .... and Mr. Choi for dinner. Tuesday at 8 PM .... And sushi ....!

I'm looking forward to our visit next week.

Kind regards,
Robert Schmidt

Dear Ms. Lee:

Thanks very much for the invitation. .... I can't join you for dinner on Tuesday evening. .... because I already have an appointment that evening.

Since we are flying back to Germany on Wednesday, ... But I hope we can have dinner together on my next visit.

Best wishes,
Christine Adams

B Work with a partner. You work as an assistant to the Marketing Director, Bill Mason. He asks you to invite a customer, Mr. Thaworn, to dinner with him on Thursday, after his visit to your company. Write the email. Use the language in 6A.

C Swap emails with another pair. Decide if you accept their invitation. Write a reply and give it to them. Use the language in 6A.

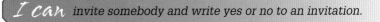

I can invite somebody and write yes or no to an invitation.

TOEIC® practice

1 Listening

A | 🔊42 **Question–Response** Listen carefully. Choose the best response to the sentence you hear.

Example: When did you last see Mai?

    A ☐ She lives in London.

    B ☑ She visited me yesterday.

    C ☐ Probably next week.

1 A ☐   B ☐   C ☐
2 A ☐   B ☐   C ☐
3 A ☐   B ☐   C ☐
4 A ☐   B ☐   C ☐

B | 🔊43 **Conversations** Listen and answer the questions.

Conversation 1

1 Who are the speakers?

  ☐ **A** husband and wife

  ☐ **B** father and daughter

  ☐ **C** business colleagues

  ☐ **D** store clerk and customer

2 Where are they having the conversation?

  ☐ **A** at the lunch table

  ☐ **B** in a store

  ☐ **C** at the dentist's

  ☐ **D** in the office

3 What's Sandy planning to do?

  ☐ **A** take her son to the dentist

  ☐ **B** go to the meeting

  ☐ **C** leave early

  ☐ **D** have lunch with Mike

Conversation 2

1 Where are the speakers?

  ☐ **A** at a travel agency

  ☐ **B** at a car-rental company

  ☐ **C** at a hotel

  ☐ **D** at the airport

2 When are the Tomlins leaving?

  ☐ **A** on June 1

  ☐ **B** on June 2

  ☐ **C** on June 3

  ☐ **D** on June 4

3 What's the problem?

  ☐ **A** Mr. Tomlin forgot to confirm.

  ☐ **B** The name Tomlin is not in the computer.

  ☐ **C** Mr. Tomlin forgot to make a reservation.

  ☐ **D** The woman is having problems with the computer.

2 Reading

Text completion Read the passage. Choose the best word to complete each sentence.

Dear Max,

I started my office job at Nanking Fashions last Monday, and I really like it. I start work **1**.......... nine o'clock every morning.

- ☐ **A** for
- ☐ **B** on
- ☐ **C** to
- ☐ **D** at

We **2**.......... lunch at one o'clock. Yesterday I **3**.......... our boss, Mr Tang.

- ☐ **A** usually have
- ☐ **B** are usually having
- ☐ **C** have usually
- ☐ **D** usually are having

- ☐ **A** did meet
- ☐ **B** met
- ☐ **C** meet
- ☐ **D** not meet

He's **4**.........., and he's very nice.

- ☐ **A** China
- ☐ **B** Chinaman
- ☐ **C** Chinese
- ☐ **D** China person

Best wishes,
Suzie

3 Writing

Respond to a written request Reply to the email. Give and ask for at least TWO more pieces of information.

From: Max Bird
To: Suzie Tseng
Subject: New job

Hi Suzie,

Thanks for your letter. It was interesting to read about your new job. Please tell me more about Nanking Fashions.

I started a new job last Monday, too. I am still with Nokia, but now I work in the head office in Helsinki.

Best wishes,
Max

Work and play

1 Business situation
During and after work

A [44] **Pham Thanh Ly from Hanoi and Amsyar Yeoh from Johor Bahru both work at a British company in Kuala Lumpur. They sometimes meet for lunch. Listen to their lunchtime conversation and check (✔) the boxes.**

Who . . .	Ly	Amsyar
1 likes meeting people?	☐	☐
2 enjoys talking to customers?	☐	☐
3 enjoys working in a team?	☐	☐
4 dislikes going to conferences?	☐	☐
5 hates giving presentations?	☐	☐
6 hates reading reports?	☐	☐
7 dislikes writing reports?	☐	☐
8 doesn't mind looking after visitors?	☐	☐

B [45] **Now listen to the rest of their conversation and complete the sentences.**

1 Amsyar prefers .... time with his family.
2 Ly is learning .... the saxophone.
3 Ly tries .... as many sports as she can.
4 Ly wants .... fit.
5 Amsyar prefers .... sports on TV.
6 Ly promised .... a report.
7 Ly wants .... the report today.
8 Amsyar hopes .... Ly again tomorrow.

▷ ▪ activity ▪ presentation
  ▪ boring ▪ leisure

I can understand a conversation about work and leisure.

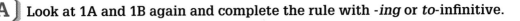

A Look at 1A and 1B again and complete the rule with *-ing* or *to*-infinitive.

> After the verbs *dislike, enjoy, hate, like,* and *mind,* we use the
> .... form of the verb.
>
> After the verbs *hope, learn, prefer, promise, try,* and *want* we
> use the .... form of the verb.

> Note the difference:
>
> *I like working in a team.* (= enjoy)
>
> *Today, I would like to finish the report.* (= want to)

B Put the verbs into the correct forms.

Miyu is a student. She enjoys **1** *traveling* (travel) and
would like **2** *to travel* (travel) around the world. She
wants **3** .... (work) for a travel agency when
she finishes college. She likes **4** .... (work)
with people, and she is trying **5** .... (learn)
English and other foreign languages.

Haruto is Miyu's boyfriend. He's different from Miyu.
He hates **6** .... (travel) and prefers
7 .... (spend) his vacations at home. But
he doesn't mind **8** .... (help) Miyu to learn
English. Haruto would like **9** .... (be) an IT
specialist, and he knows that English is important.

C Work with a partner. Ask and answer questions about your activities. Use the
words and phrases in the boxes.

(don't) like	on the weekend
dislike	in the evening
(don't) enjoy	on Monday morning
don't mind	early in the morning
hate	during the rainy season
hope	next year
prefer	

A: *What do you enjoy doing on the weekend?*
B: *I enjoy sleeping late. What about you?*
A: *I enjoy . . .*

▷ ▪ travel agency ▪ foreign
  ▪ specialist

I can use *-ing* and *to*-infinitive forms after some verbs.

D 44 45 **Connecting words are words that join sentences. In 1A Ly says:**

I like meeting people, **and** I enjoy talking to customers.
That's great, **but** there has to be something you don't like.

Listen to the conversations again. Check (✔) the connecting words you hear.

☐ because   ☐ so
☐ if   ☐ than

> We usually put a comma before *but* and *so*, but not before *because* and *than*:
>
> I'm sorry, but I'm too busy.
>
> He speaks English because he lived there for many years.

E **Underline the correct word.**

1 Amsyar likes his job **because / so** it's interesting.
2 Li wants to stay fit, **so / but** she spends a lot of time at the gym.
3 Amsyar watches sports on TV, **than / but** he doesn't watch movies.
4 Li is a faster driver **than / and** I am.
5 You can have lunch with me **because / if** you want to.
6 We can have dinner **and / but** then go to a movie.

F **Write six sentences from the chart. Use each connecting word only once. Add commas when necessary.**

1 I wrote a report	and	my boss asked me to do it.
2 I wrote the report	because	the one I wrote last week.
3 The report is finished	but	I had to write it again.
4 My boss didn't like the report	if	you want me to.
	so	my boss liked it.
5 It was a longer report	than	my boss doesn't like it
6 I can write a report		

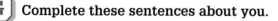

I wrote a report, and my boss liked it.

G **Complete these sentences about you.**

1 I am learning English because ....
2 I am learning English, but ....
3 I need to practice my English, so ....
4 I want to speak better English than ....

I can use connecting words.

3 Listening and speaking
Travel and leisure in Asia

A 〔46〕 Lillian Majid works for a company called International Leisure Services. Listen to the radio interview. Match the countries with the leisure activities.

1 China	....	**A**	theme parks
2 Indonesia	....	**B**	health spas
3 Thailand	....	**C**	the golf industry

B 〔46〕 Listen to the interview again and complete the sentences.

1 International Leisure Services is located in ....
2 The company .... health spas, golf clubs, and theme parks.
3 Visitors from all over the world come to Thailand to do something for ....
4 Many golfers prefer to play golf in China because it's ....
5 In the Bali water park you can swim and take part in ....
6 The .... industry is a trillion-dollar industry worldwide.

C Work with a partner.

Student A: Go to Partner file 7.
Student B: Look at the information below. Ask Student A questions and fill in the missing information.

Legoland Malaysia is located
.... (where?). It opened
.... (when?). It's special
because .... (why?).
.... (who?) built it,
and it cost .... (how
much?). It has over ....
(how many?) rides, shows, and attractions.
There is a very big store that sells
.... (what?). Legoland
Malaysia has about ....
(how many?) visitors a year.

Now answer Student A's questions with information from the text below.

Hong Kong Disneyland is located on Lantau Island. The park opened to visitors on September 12, 2005. It's special because it was the first Disneyland to focus on Chinese culture. The Walt Disney company and the government of Hong Kong own the theme park. Hong Kong Disneyland has over five million visitors a year. You can visit seven different theme areas there. A day ticket costs between HK$100 and HK$450.

▷ ▪ health ▪ to take part in ▪ fantastic
▪ entertainment ▪ located in

I can understand and talk about travel and leisure in Asia.

Vocabulary focus
Focus 1: *play/do/go . . .*

A **[47]** Listen to the conversation and put the words in the correct group.

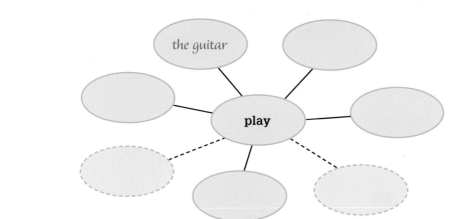

| aerobics | computer games | golf | ~~shopping~~ |
| ~~aerobics~~ | | | |

aerobics   computer games   golf   ~~shopping~~
swimming   backpacking   cycling   jogging
skiing   ~~the guitar~~   chess   soccer   karate
sports   weight training

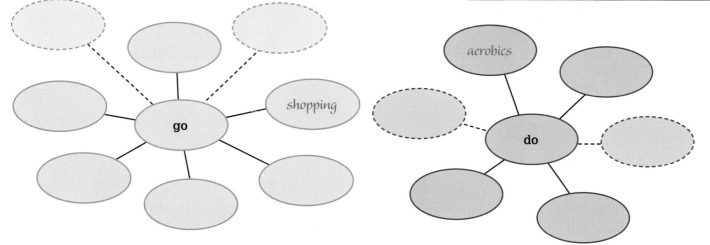

the guitar

play

go   shopping

aerobics   **do**

Complete the rule with *play*, *do*, or *go*.

We often use .... with activities that end in *-ing*.
We often use .... with games.
We use .... with many other sports.

Add two more words of your own to each group.

B Work with a partner. Which of the activities in 4A does your partner do?
Ask where and when your partner does these things.

A: *Do you play the guitar?*
B: *No, I don't. Do you do aerobics?*
A: *Yes, I do.*
B: *Where do you do aerobics?*
A: *In a gym.*
B: *When do you do aerobics?*
A: *Twice a week, on Mondays and Wednesdays.*

Vocabulary focus

Focus 2: Describing leisure activities

C Look at the words below. Are they positive or negative? Make a chart and put them in the correct column.

| a waste of time | dangerous | difficult | exciting | fun | hectic |
| boring | easy | (too) expensive | great | interesting |

(a waste of time and easy are crossed out)

🙂 **Positive**	🙁 **Negative**
easy . . .	*a waste of time . . .*

D Work with a partner. Name the activities in the pictures. Then talk about the things you like and don't like. Use the words in 4C.

| boxing | dancing | having a barbecue | listening to music |
| playing computer games | playing tennis | skateboarding | traveling |

1   2   3   4

5   6   7   8

A: *Do you like skateboarding?*

B: *Yes. I like skateboarding because it's fun. Do you like boxing?*

A: *No, I don't. It's too dangerous, but I like watching it on TV.*

E ▷ **Key words** Look at the words at the bottom of pages 73–76. Choose the best words to complete the sentences.

1 Ly hates giving .... because she is always nervous.
2 The opposite of interesting is ....
3 Do you .... in any sports .... ?
4 Miyu wants to travel to .... countries.
5 The theme park offers games and ....
6 People go to spas to do something for their ....
7 I didn't organize my trip myself. A .... organized it.
8 I enjoyed my trip to the theme park. It was .... !

I can talk about my leisure time activities.

Reading
Tourists in Thailand

A) **Before you read** What do you know about the tourist industry in your country? Where do the tourists come from? What do they want to see?

Asian Business **Online**
looks at Chinese tourists in Thailand.

Thailand is an attractive destination for tourists from all over the world. But in the last few years, it has become very popular with the mainland Chinese.

The boom of Chinese tourists in Thailand started with Xu Zheng's 2012 movie *Lost in Thailand*. The comedy is about two Chinese businessmen who go to Thailand to find their boss. The movie was an enormous hit in China, and only one year later a quarter of a million Chinese tourists visited Thailand. And that was only the beginning!

Of course, the tourist boom in Thailand is not only the result of the movie. Another important reason is that more and more airlines are offering low-cost flights to Bangkok from large Chinese cities. This means that flying to Thailand is now possible for low-income travelers. A third reason is that Thailand offers tourists visas when they arrive. This makes it easier to plan a short trip because you don't need to get a visa before you leave home.

This year the Tourism Authority of Thailand expects that 15 percent of its 25 million tourists will come from mainland China. As well as the traditional tourist destinations such as Bangkok, Pattaya, and Phuket, the Chinese often choose to visit Chiang Mai. Why? Because *Lost in Thailand* shows this beautiful place at its best.

Thanks, Xu Zheng!

B) **The main idea** Find and correct four mistakes in the text below.

In 2012, a quarter of a million Chinese tourists visited Thailand. They all came as a result of the movie *Lost in Thailand*. Flying to Thailand is more expensive than in the past. Tourists to Thailand have to get a visa before they leave.

C) **Comprehension**

1 What is the movie *Lost in Thailand* about?
2 Why is Thailand now attractive for low-income travelers?
3 What makes it easier for the Chinese to plan a trip to Thailand?
4 Why is Chiang Mai a popular destination with the Chinese?

D) **Now you** An English-speaking friend asked about your country. Write and tell him/her about . . .

- the most popular and/or famous destinations
- the things he/she should see and why
- the things he/she can do and where
- the places he/she can stay
- the food he/she should try

 I can understand a text about tourism in Thailand.

Culture focus
Body language in Asia

A Body language in business situations is different from country to country.

EYE CONTACT In China, it's important to look somebody in the eyes and keep eye contact. But in Indonesia, people feel uncomfortable if you look into their eyes for too long. In South Korea, you can make eye contact with younger people, but you can't with older people. It's a question of respect.

GESTURES Malaysians use their hands a lot when they are talking, but the Japanese do not. In some countries, for example in Thailand, you mustn't point your finger at someone. In South Korea, teachers expect students to hand in their papers with both hands. It's more polite.

DISTANCE Filipinos keep more distance than people in many other Asian countries do. In Malaysia and Thailand, for example, people often stand very close to each other. People in Taiwan also stand close, but not when they are talking to a boss or manager. Here they keep their distance to show respect.

TOUCHING In Thailand and Laos, you mustn't touch people you don't know well, and you must never touch anyone on the head. In South Korea, you can touch other people. Men often touch each other more than in other Asian countries.

SHAKING HANDS In China and India both men and women shake hands. But when you first meet a woman in Malaysia, you mustn't offer your hand. Wait and see if she does first. In Thailand you don't shake hands but "wai" instead.

B Underline the correct country. In which country can you . . .

1	touch a business partner?	Korea / Laos
2	offer your hand to a woman?	India / Malaysia
3	make and keep eye contact?	Indonesia / China
4	stand very close to the person you're talking to?	Philippines / Malaysia
5	use your hands a lot when you're talking?	Malaysia / Japan

C In which country is it not polite to . . .

1 touch a person's head? ....
2 point a finger at someone? ....
3 give somebody something with one hand? ....
4 make eye contact with an older person? ....
5 stand close to your boss? ....

D Work with a partner. Make a list of body language rules for your country.

😀 Polite	🙁 Not polite

I can understand body language in Asian countries.

Come again soon!

1 Business situation
Saying goodbye

A | 〔48〕 **After his business trip to Bangkok, Tony Marshall is returning to Sydney. He is saying goodbye to his business partner, Chermarn Arak. Listen to the conversation and underline the correct answers.**

1 Tony's flight leaves in the **morning** / **evening**.
2 Tony will arrive in Sydney at **a quarter to seven** / **half past six**.
3 Tony will take **a taxi** / **a bus** from the airport.
4 The long flight is **a problem** / **no problem** for Tony.
5 Tony thanks Chermarn for **the meeting** / **her help**.
6 Tony gives Chermarn **a book** / **some chocolates**.
7 Tony says he'll be **in touch** / **in Sydney**.

B | 〔48〕 **Below are some useful phrases for saying goodbye. Listen again and complete the sentences.**

1 It was .... to meet you.
2 It was a .... for me, too.
3 .... you'll visit us again soon.
4 Please give my regards to ....
5 Have a .... home.
6 Please .... soon.
7 I'll be in ....

▷ ▪ pleasure ▪ regards ▪ in touch

I can *understand people saying goodbye.*

Grammar focus

Focus 1: The *will*-future

A Listen to the first part of the conversation and complete it with **'ll**, **will**, or **won't** and the correct verb from the box.

| ~~arrive~~ | be (2x) | land | read | sleep | take |

Chermarn: When **1** *will you arrive* home?

Tony: We **2** .... at about a quarter to seven tomorrow morning. I hope we **3** .... late. I **4** .... a taxi from the airport, and I **5** .... home about nine o'clock.

Chermarn: Oh, that's a long trip.

Tony: It's no problem. I **6** .... much, but I **7** .... and play computer games.

B Complete the rule.

> We use *will* to talk about the future.
> The short form is .... The negative is ....

C Read about Cindy. Then work with a partner and answer the questions.

> Cindy works in an office. She works from 8:30 AM to 4:30 PM every day.
> It's 9 AM and Cindy **is** in the office.
> At 9 AM yesterday she **was** in the office.
> At 9 AM tomorrow she **will be** in the office.

1 What time is it where you are? Tell your partner . . .
  – where you were at this time yesterday.
  – where you will be at this time tomorrow.

2 Ask and answer questions about these times:
  – at eight o'clock yesterday evening
  – at midnight tonight
  – at six o'clock this evening
  – in one year from now
  – last Saturday afternoon
  – next Saturday afternoon

A: *Where were you at eight o'clock yesterday evening?*
B: *I was in a café with a friend.*
A: *Where will you be at midnight tonight?*
B: *I'm not sure. I'll probably be in bed!*

> You can give short answers like this:
>
> **A:** *Will you be in the office tomorrow?*   **A:** *Will you be on a trip?*
> **B:** *No, I won't.*   **B:** *Yes, I will.*

⸱ probably

▷

I can use will *and* won't *to talk about the future.*

D Can you remember the grammar from Units 1 to 10? Try this quiz. There is one point for every correct answer.

1 Where .... on Mondays?
- [ ] **A** Huan goes
- [ ] **B** does Huan go
- [ ] **C** goes Huan

2 .... any files in your office?
- [ ] **A** Is there
- [ ] **B** Are they
- [ ] **C** Are there

3 Ly .... green tea.
- [ ] **A** never drinks
- [ ] **B** doesn't never drink
- [ ] **C** drinks never

4 Look! Kasem .... lunch with Mai.
- [ ] **A** has
- [ ] **B** had
- [ ] **C** is having

5 We don't have .... smartphones on sale this week.
- [ ] **A** any
- [ ] **B** some
- [ ] **C** none

6 Where .... your next vacation?
- [ ] **A** do you spend
- [ ] **B** are you spending
- [ ] **C** you spend

7 My colleagues are all .... me.
- [ ] **A** more older than
- [ ] **B** older than
- [ ] **C** older as

8 What time .... at the office this morning?
- [ ] **A** did you arrive
- [ ] **B** arrived you
- [ ] **C** do you arrive

9 You .... smoke in the office. It's not allowed.
- [ ] **A** don't need to
- [ ] **B** have to
- [ ] **C** mustn't

10 Miyu enjoys .... to her colleagues.
- [ ] **A** talk
- [ ] **B** to talk
- [ ] **C** talking

11 Amsyar is studying hard .... he wants to be an engineer.
- [ ] **A** so
- [ ] **B** because
- [ ] **C** but

12 I .... in a meeting all day tomorrow.
- [ ] **A** will probably be
- [ ] **B** probably will be
- [ ] **C** probably am

Score
11–12 points: Very good
9–10 points: Good
7–8 points: OK
0–7 points: Practice!

3 Listening and speaking
The workplace in 2025

A 🔊49 Listen to Sora Kim interviewing Chen Ming about his book, *The 2025 Workplace*. Are the statements true or false? Correct the false statements.

	True	False
1 Chen says there will be more "remote working."		
2 A few people will work in virtual offices.		
3 Employees will travel thousands of miles to work on projects.		
4 It will be important to visit your company's office.		
5 You will sometimes communicate with avatars.		
6 Web-conferencing and 3D avatars will be expensive.		
7 Companies will spend more money on offices and equipment.		
8 Everyone will work 24/7 in the future.		

B 🔊50 **Talking about ...** the future

Step 1: Listen to two people talking about the future. How certain are their ideas? Complete what they say with *definitely* or *probably*.

Sanda Myint, office worker, Myanmar

"I like my job, so I'll **1** .... stay with this company for as long as I can. The company also has an office in the United States, so I'll **2** .... work there for a year or two, but I'll **3** .... come back to Myanmar. I'll **4** .... get married and have children one day, but I **5** .... want to continue working after I'm married."

Saiful Muhamat, assistant sales manager, Malaysia

"I **6** .... want to travel. My company is growing, so I'll **7** .... travel to Europe some time in the next few years. If I do, I'll **8** .... take my family with me. Later I'll **9** .... study some more and get a better degree – perhaps an MBA."

Step 2: Think about your future and make some notes.

Step 3: Work with a partner. Tell each other about your future.

I guess / I'm sure . . .   *I'll definitely/probably . . .*
I expect/hope/think I'll . . .   *I definitely/probably won't . . .*

▷ ▪ remote ▪ trend ▪ project
▪ touch screen ▪ 24/7 ▪ definitely

I can listen to and talk about life in the future.

Vocabulary focus
Focus 1: Saying hello and goodbye

A Make a chart and put the phrases into the correct column.

~~Have a good trip.~~   I'll be in touch.
~~Hi, how are you?~~   It was a pleasure.
How do you do?   Nice to meet you.
How was the weather in Sydney?   Please give them my regards.
How was the trip?   Thanks for everything.
I hope to see you again soon.   This is my colleague, Robert.

Saying hello	Saying goodbye
Hi, how are you? . . .	*Have a good trip . . .*

B Match the sentences in a conversation.

1 How was the trip?	E	**A** Yes, I'll do that.
2 How do you do?	....	**B** You're welcome.
3 Please give them my regards.	....	**C** Nice to meet you.
4 Thanks for everything.	....	**D** Fine thanks. And you?
5 This is my colleague, Robert.	....	**E** ~~OK, just very long.~~
6 Hi, how are you?	....	**F** How do you do?

C 〔49〕 Listen to the conversation from 3A again and fill in the missing prepositions.

1 I'd like to welcome you .... our program.
2 Today I'm talking .... Chen Ming .... his book.
3 The book looks .... the question "What will work be like in the future?"
4 Employees will work together .... projects.
5 Companies won't spend any money .... office buildings and equipment.
6 That depends .... you.

D Put the words in the correct order and give the missing preposition.

1 can / again / look / problem / the / we ? *Can we look at the problem again?*
2 it / the / depends / weather ....
3 I'd / our / welcome / to / you / like / company ....
4 I / all / money / my / new / spent / software ....
5 now / presentation / working / my / I'm ....
6 what / to / you / do / want / today / talk ? ....

E ▷ **Key words** Look at the words at the bottom of pages 81–84. Choose the best words to complete the sentences.

1 Please give my .... to your colleagues.
2 This store is open ....
3 A large team is working on this ....
4 It was a .... to meet you.
5 I'll be .... by phone as soon as possible.
6 If something is " .... " it's a long way away.
7 The new smartphone has an unbreakable ....
8 Mia likes to follow the latest fashion ....

> *I can* *say hello and goodbye and use prepositions after verbs.*

F Can you remember the vocabulary from Units 1 to 10? Try this quiz. There is one point for every correct answer.

Part 1 Complete the sentences with the correct word.

1 The official language of Vietnam is ....
2 The opposite of "difficult" is ....
3 The word used in the International Telephone Alphabet for V is ....
4 A telephone number for another country always begins with the ....
5 The second month of the year is ....
6 We throw things we don't want into the ....
7 Sorry, he isn't in the office. Can I take a ....?
8 A person who works in a store is a ....

Part 2 Choose the correct answer.

9 I'm traveling .... business.
   ☐ **A** for
   ☐ **B** on
   ☐ **C** in

10 Ms. Cheng is talking on the other ....
   ☐ **A** desk.
   ☐ **B** room.
   ☐ **C** line.

11 The bookstore is .... the pharmacy.
   ☐ **A** across from
   ☐ **B** straight on
   ☐ **C** left of

12 Huang sometimes .... jogging after work.
   ☐ **A** does
   ☐ **B** goes
   ☐ **C** plays

13 My family always gives gifts .... Christmas.
   ☐ **A** in
   ☐ **B** to
   ☐ **C** at

14 Can I .... a reservation?
   ☐ **A** do
   ☐ **B** make
   ☐ **C** book

Part 3 Complete each sentence with one of the key words from the box.

| compare | department | leisure | presentation | repeat | reservation |

15 I didn't understand. Could you .... that, please?
16 I have a .... for a double room.
17 Ly works in the marketing ....
18 Hui and Hina always .... prices.
19 The .... industry is growing very fast.
20 The .... was really interesting.

Score

18–20 points: Very good
15–17 points: Good
12–14 points: OK
0–12 points: Practice!

Reading
The ASEAN Economic Community

A) **Before you read** How many countries are in the ASEAN? Can you name them?

Asian Business **Online**
talks to three people about the ASEAN Economic Community (AEC).

Benigno Estrada, an engineer from Manila, Philippines
One advantage of the AEC, of course, is that things from other member countries will be cheaper. But the most exciting thing for me is that I'll be able to work in all ASEAN countries. I can go where the conditions are good and where I can earn a good salary. Some people are worried that all the skilled people will leave the poor countries and go to the rich countries. But, in my opinion, people must decide for themselves where they want to go and work.

Chanya Seng, a businesswoman from Phnom Penh, Cambodia
For me the AEC will mean I can save time. For businesspeople "time is money," so for me the ASEAN Business Travel Card is a great idea. Business travelers who have the Travel Card won't need visas to travel between ASEAN countries. With the Travel Card I'll save valuable time at the borders. I'll be able to use special fast-track immigration, and I won't have to stand in line for long.

Le Dinh Tung, a student from Ho Chi Minh City, Vietnam
I'm sure the AEC will mean better job opportunities for me personally. I'm studying English as my major, and this will be a great advantage for me. English will be important in the ASEAN community. Some ASEAN countries already use English as their official language, and some use English as their second language, so English will certainly be the language they use to communicate with each other. Also I love traveling, so I'm really pleased that traveling from one country to another will be so much easier.

B) **The main idea** Skim the text to find who talks about . . .

1 easier business travel. ....
2 communication between ASEAN countries. ....
3 better jobs in different countries. ....

C) **Scanning for detail** Are the statements correct? If not, correct them.

1 The most important thing for Benigno Estrada is that things will be cheaper.
2 Benigno Estrada is worried that skilled people will leave his country.
3 Chanya Seng wants to spend less time when traveling.
4 Someone with a Travel Card won't have to wait so long at Immigration.
5 Le Dinh Tung will have no personal advantage from ASEAN.
6 Le Dinh Tung thinks his major will be very useful.

D) **Now you** Will ASEAN be important for you? Why?

> *I can* understand an article about the advantages of the ASEAN Economic Community.

6 Business writing
A thank-you email

A When Tony Marshall returns to his office in Sydney, he sends Chermarn Arak an email to thank her.

What are the phrases Tony uses to . . .

1 describe his journey?
2 talk about the future?
3 say thank you?
4 say he enjoyed meeting Chermarn?
5 say something personal?

> Dear Chermarn,
>
> Thank you very much for your kind welcome and the useful meeting we had in Bangkok.
>
> My return flight to Sydney was fine, and we arrived on time.
>
> It was very nice to meet you personally, and I hope we can work together again soon.
>
> Remember we talked about barbecues – or "barbies" as we say in Australia? Well, here's a picture of me in my backyard.
>
> I look forward to seeing you again – perhaps in Sydney!
>
> Best wishes,
> Tony

B You were on a business trip to Sydney. Your business partner there was Tony Marshall. Now you are back in your office. Write a letter of thanks.

○ Describe your journey.
○ Say thank you.
○ Say you enjoyed seeing Tony again.
○ Say something personal.
○ Talk about the future.

Thanks!

C **An email quiz** Choose the correct word and put it into the correct form.

1 I .... (receive / reply) your email yesterday.
2 Please find .... (attach / link) details of our courses.
3 Please .... (do / send) me some more information.
4 I would like .... (confirm / contact) your reservation.
5 We are looking forward to .... (find / meet) you.

I can write a thank-you email.

TOEIC® practice

1 Listening

A) 🔊51 **Photographs** Listen. Then choose the sentence that best describes the photograph.

1 A ☐ B ☐ C ☐ D ☐   2 A ☐ B ☐ C ☐ D ☐

B) 🔊52 **Talks** You will hear a phone call message. Choose the best answer to each question.

1 Who does the caller want to speak to?

☐ **A** Tony Marshall   ☐ **B** Sandy James   ☐ **C** Suki Smith   ☐ **D** Eddie Johnson

2 What is the reason for the message?

☐ **A** to suggest a different place for the meeting
☐ **B** to explain why the caller can't come to the meeting
☐ **C** to change the date of the meeting
☐ **D** to cancel the meeting

3 The caller would prefer to have the meeting on

☐ **A** Monday.   ☐ **B** Wednesday.   ☐ **C** Thursday.   ☐ **D** Friday.

2 Speaking

A) **Describe a picture** Choose one of the pictures in 1A. Look at it for 30 seconds, then describe it in your own words.

B) **Read a text aloud** You have 45 seconds to look at the text below. Then you have 45 seconds to read it aloud.

> A new report on the future of travel shows that there will be a big increase in "do-it-yourself" travel – that means that travelers will organize their trips themselves. They will use social media sites, forums, and online communities in the way that travelers in the past used a travel agent. Travel agencies will not disappear, but the way they communicate with their customers will change. For example, they will allow mobile transactions or transactions through social media sites.

3 Reading

Incomplete sentences Choose the best word or phrase to complete each sentence.

1 I enjoy .... after a hard day's work.

- ☐ **A** to relax
- ☐ **B** relax
- ☐ **C** relaxing
- ☐ **D** relaxes

2 What kinds of sports do you prefer to .... at the weekend.

- ☐ **A** do
- ☐ **B** have
- ☐ **C** make
- ☐ **D** enjoy

3 I .... at the meeting on Friday.

- ☐ **A** won't be probably
- ☐ **B** won't probably be
- ☐ **C** will be probably not
- ☐ **D** probably won't be

4 I am looking forward .... you again soon.

- ☐ **A** to see
- ☐ **B** to seeing
- ☐ **C** that I see
- ☐ **D** see

5 Please give my .... to your colleagues.

- ☐ **A** regards
- ☐ **B** wishes
- ☐ **C** greetings
- ☐ **D** hopes

6 It all depends .... the weather.

- ☐ **A** from
- ☐ **B** to
- ☐ **C** on
- ☐ **D** by

4 Writing

Write a sentence based on a picture Write ONE sentence based on each picture. Use the two words or phrases that are given with the picture.

Example: picnic / next weekend
Possible answer:
Kim and her friends will have a picnic in the park next weekend.

1 morning / crowd

2 new technologies / future workplace

Partner files

Partner file 1

Unit 2   2C

Student A: Look at the picture below.

You each have a picture of the same office, but on different days. There are 10 differences. Can you find them? Take turns to ask questions.

Is there a . . . in your picture?
Are there any . . . in your picture?
How many . . . ?
Where . . . ?
What color . . . ?

files	printer	plant
bookcase	desk	empty
full	lamp	calculator
notepad	trash can	

Partner file 2

Unit 3   2D

Student A: Look at these activities. Pretend you're doing these things:

brush your hair	eat a sandwich	play the guitar	listen to music	welcome a visitor

Try to guess what your partner is doing. Take turns asking and answering questions.

Think of other activities to show your partner.

> Are you .... ing?

> Yes, I'm .... ing.

> No, I'm not .... ing.

Partner file 3

Unit 4   2D

Student A: Ask your partner about things he/she has in his/her office. Ask about:

books	coffee	money	paper clips	pens	plants	printer paper	tea

Do you have any books in your office?

Look at the pictures below of things you have and don't have in your office. Answer your partner's questions.

Yes, I have some coffee in my office. No, I don't have any flash drives.

markers ✔   folders ✔   tea ✘   notepads ✘

coffee ✔   milk ✔   plants ✘   flash drives ✘

Partner file 4

Unit 5   2E

Student A: You have Dr. Little's agenda for next week, but some of the information is missing. Ask Student B for the missing information and answer your partner's questions. Use these verbs:

fly   have   leave   stay (2x)

A: *Where is Dr. Little flying to on Monday?*
B: *He's . . .*

July

15 Monday	– Flight CZ 7976 – 10 PM Manila – .... *(where to?)*
16 Tuesday	– 10 AM arrive London – two nights in .... *(where?)*
17 Wednesday	– 10:30 AM meet David Johnson
18 Thursday	– .... *(what time?)* lunch with Marion Smith – 3 PM take train to Liverpool – .... *(which?)* Hotel
19 Friday	– 10 AM attend workshop – Flight CZ 7934 – .... *(what time?)* Liverpool – London – Manila
20 Saturday	– 11 PM arrive Manila

Partner file 5

Unit 6   1C

Student A: Prepare a conversation with your partner. Then read it to the class.

– You work as a reservations clerk at the Plaza Hotel.
– A customer has a reservation for a double room for three nights, May 21–24.
– The customer calls to ask if it is possible to stay one extra night.

– You have no double rooms for that night. Offer two single rooms.
– The special price for the two rooms is $150.
– You can confirm the reservation by email.

A: *The Plaza Hotel. How can I help you?*
B: *Hello. My name is . . . I have a reservation for . . .*

Partner file 6

Student A:

1 Describe this picture to your partner.

2 Look at pictures C and D. Which picture is your partner describing?

C

D

Partner file 7

Student A: Look at the information below. Student B will ask you some questions.

Legoland Malaysia is located near Johor Bahru. It opened in September 2012. It is special because it was the first Legoland theme park in Asia. A British company built it, and it cost US$230 million. It has over 40 rides, shows, and attractions. There is a very big store that sells Lego products such as toys, books, and DVDs. Legoland Malaysia has about 1.5 million visitors a year.

Now ask Student B questions and fill in the missing information.

Hong Kong Disneyland is located on .... (*where?*). The park opened to visitors .... (*when?*). It's special because .... (*why?*). .... (*who?*) own the theme park. Hong Kong Disneyland has .... (*how many?*) visitors a year. You can visit .... (*what?*) there. A day ticket costs .... (*how much?*).

Irregular verbs

Infinitive	Past simple	Past participle ("3rd form")
be	was/were	been
beat	beat	beaten
become	became	become
begin	began	begun
bite	bit	bitten
break	broke	broken
build	built	built
buy	bought	bought
can	could	–
catch	caught	caught
choose	chose	chosen
come	came	come
cut	cut	cut
do	did	done
drive	drove	driven
eat	ate	eaten
fall	fell	fallen
feel	felt	felt
find	found	found
fly	flew	flown
get	got	got/gotten
give	gave	given
go	went	gone
grow	grew	grown
have	had	had
hear	heard	heard
hit	hit	hit
hurt	hurt	hurt

Infinitive	Past simple	Past participle ("3rd form")
keep	kept	kept
know	knew	known
leave	left	left
lose	lost	lost
make	made	made
meet	met	met
put	put	put
read	read	read
ride	rode	ridden
run	ran	run
say	said	said
see	saw	seen
sell	sold	sold
send	sent	sent
sit	sat	sat
sleep	slept	slept
speak	spoke	spoken
stand	stood	stood
swim	swam	swum
take	took	taken
teach	taught	taught
tell	told	told
think	thought	thought
throw	threw	thrown
understand	understood	understood
wake	woke	woken
win	won	won
write	wrote	written

Transcripts

Unit 1

Track 1

Mr. Akimoto: Excuse me. Are you Robert Tomlin?
Mr. Tomlin: Yes, that's right.
Mr. Akimoto: Good morning, Mr. Tomlin. I'm Hiroshi Akimoto from GameZ. Welcome to Osaka.
Mr. Tomlin: Thank you. Nice to meet you, Mr. Akimoto. This is my colleague Christine Klein.
Ms. Klein: Nice to meet you, Mr. Akimoto.
Mr. Akimoto: Nice to meet you, too, Ms. Klein. Can I help you with your bags?
Ms. Klein: That's very kind.
Mr. Akimoto: How was your flight?
Mr. Tomlin: It was pretty long, but it was fine.
Mr. Akimoto: So let's go. My car's outside.

Track 2

1 **A:** Excuse me. Are you Ms. Lee?
　B: Yes, that's right. You must be Mr. Tang.
　A: Yes, I am. I'm sorry to keep you waiting.
　B: That's all right.

2 **A:** Are you going to Indonesia on business?
　B: Yes, I am. And you?
　A: No, I'm going on vacation.
　B: Lucky you!

Track 3

B: Is this your first trip to Indonesia?
A: Yes, I usually spend my vacations in Europe. And you?
B: This is my second time.
A: Do you like it there?
B: Oh, yes. The people are friendly, and the food is good.

A: What sort of things do they eat there?
B: A lot of fruit and fish. Do you like that kind of food?
A: Yes, I do. And does everyone speak English?
B: Well, not everyone. But it isn't difficult to find somebody who does.

Track 4

1 **A:** Well, it was nice to talk to you.
　B: Yes, I hope we can meet again sometime.
　A: That would be great. I'll call you next time I'm in town.
　B: Fine.

2 **A:** Would you excuse me? I have to go soon.
　B: What time does your plane leave?
　A: At six. So I really have to hurry.
　B: No problem. Shall I call you a taxi?

Track 5

1 Would passengers for flight number MH 537 to Bangkok please go to Gate E15?
2 Flight SQ 261 to Singapore leaves from Gate A39.
3 Flight UA 9679 to Chicago is now boarding at Gate B30.
4 All Nippon Airways flight NH 489 to Jakarta leaves from Gate D5.
5 Would passengers for flight LH 3379 to London please go to Gate G8?
6 Flight TK 1789 to Istanbul is now boarding at Gate C12.

Track 6

Phone call 1
A: Hello, this is Robert Tomlin. Could I speak to Mr. Akimoto, please?
B: I'm sorry, he's not in the office at the moment. Can I take a message?
A: Yes. Tell him I'm in Osaka, and he can reach me at the Hilton at 06-6347-7111.

Phone call 2

A: Hello. This is Christine Klein. Could I speak to Ms. Chen, please?

B: I'm sorry, she's not here at the moment. Can I take a message?

A: Yes. Please tell her that I have some new information. She can call me in London at 0044 871 527 864.

Phone call 3

A: Good morning. This is the Palace Hotel, Bangkok. Miti Arak speaking. Could I speak to Ms. Otaka?

B: I'm afraid she's on vacation today. But she'll be back tomorrow. Can I take a message?

A: Yes. Could you tell her the room is booked? If she has any questions, she can call me at 02-2712-6543.

Phone call 4

A: Hi. This is Cintya Dewi. Could I speak to Yoshio Tani, please?

B: Sorry, Cintya, Yoshio's not in today. But I can take a message.

A: Thanks. Tell him my fax is OK again, and he can send me the documents. The number is 0062 2993 8876.

Track 7

My mother was born in France, my father in Spain, and they met on vacation in Mexico. I was born in Great Britain, but we also lived in the United States and Canada because my father worked there.

I love traveling, especially to Asia. I have been to Japan, Thailand, and South Korea. I would like to go to China, too. But my next vacation will be in South America, Brazil and Peru.

The only place that doesn't interest me much is Antarctica. I think it would be too cold!

Unit 2

Track 8

Robert Tomlin, product manager at Digital Design in London, England

"I am glad that I have my own office. My office is very small, but there's a desk, a chair, and a file cabinet in it. I like my one-person office. It's quiet here. In an open-plan office there's always a lot of noise. You can hear everything when your colleagues are on the phone. And it's often hectic because people walk about. And you can often waste a lot of time because colleagues want to chat. In my own office, I can keep the window open all day if I want. I have more freedom in a one-person office.

Lin Yao Chen, IT data scientist at GameZ in Osaka, Japan

"I work in an open-plan office, and I really like it. There are ten colleagues in my office, and it's so easy to communicate. I can see very quickly if someone is not in the office. I don't want to be alone in a small room, where there are only four walls to look at, and there's no one to talk to. I like to have my colleagues around me, and it's no problem for me if it's a bit noisy and hectic. An open-plan office is also much cheaper for the company because each person only needs a small place.

Track 9

Interview 1

Interviewer: So Cintya. You are a web designer, and you work for a company in Jakarta. Tell us about your typical day. What time do you get up in the morning?

Cintya: I always get up at seven o'clock, and I leave for work at eight. There's a lot of traffic at that time of the day, and it takes me about an hour and a half to get to the office.

Interviewer: What's the first thing you usually do when you get to work?

Cintya: I make coffee and then turn on the computer.

Interviewer: Where do you have lunch?

Cintya: I usually have lunch at my desk.

Interviewer: How often do you travel on business?

Cintya: I never travel on business.

Interviewer: What do you do at night?

Cintya: I have two little children. My mother takes care of them during the day, so I like to spend time with them at night.

Interviewer: Thanks for the interview, Cintya.

Interview 2

Interviewer: Mike, I know you are a sales manager for Southeast Asia. Tell us about your typical day. What time do you get up in the morning?

Mike: Well, I don't often need more than six hours of sleep, so I'm usually up by six-thirty and at my desk by seven-thirty.

Interviewer: What's the first thing you usually do when you get to work?

Mike: First I have a meeting with my team. Then I check my email. There're always some I have to answer quickly.

Interviewer: Where do you usually have lunch?

Mike: I always have lunch in the company cafeteria.

Interviewer: How often do you travel on business?

Mike: I travel a lot. I often visit different sales offices in Southeast Asia.

Interviewer: What do you do in the evenings?

Mike: Well, I often have to stay in the office late. In the evenings there are often conference calls with the main office in the US.

Interviewer: Thanks for talking with me, Mike.

Interview 3

Interviewer: Kitty Wang, you work for a fashion company in Shanghai. Tell us about your typical day. What time do you get up in the morning?

Kitty: I usually get up at seven-thirty. I always start work at nine.

Interviewer: What is the first thing you usually do when you get to work?

Kitty: I check in with my colleagues, then I go to my computer to check my email.

Interviewer: Where do you eat lunch?

Kitty: I usually eat lunch with my colleagues in a café near the office. There's a nice café just around the corner.

Interviewer: How often do you travel on business?

Kitty: About three times a year. I always go to the fashion shows in Paris, Milan, and London.

Interviewer: What do you do in the evenings?

Kitty: Not a lot. I'm usually too tired.

Interviewer: Thanks, Kitty.

Track 10

1 **A** The people are waiting for a train.
  B The people are at a busy airport.
  C There are a lot of people in the shopping mall.
  D A lot of people are boarding a plane.

2 **A** The people are exchanging business cards.
  B The people are celebrating.
  C The people are meeting and greeting.
  D The people look very unhappy.

Track 11

Example: When is your next holiday?
  A In May.
  B Last week.
  C On Bali.

1 Can I help you with your bags?
  A Yes, it is.
  B That's right.
  C That's very kind.

2 How are you?
  A Fine thanks.
  B How do you do?
  C I'm your new colleague.

3 Do you know when the plane leaves?
  A She's leaving now.
  B At 8:05, as far as I know.
  C The flight was fine.

4 Are there any emails in your in-box?
   A Yes, they are.
   B Yes, there is.
   C Yes, there are.

Unit 3

Track 12

Phone call 1

Woman: Singapore Software Systems, James Neo's secretary speaking. How can I help you?

Hiroshi: This is Hiroshi Akimoto calling from Osaka. Can I speak to Mr. Neo, please?

Woman: Yes, of course. I'll put you through.

Woman: Oh, I'm sorry, Mr. Akimoto. Mr. Neo is talking on the other line at the moment. Can he call you back?

Hiroshi: Well, I have to leave the office in a few minutes. Can I leave a message?

Woman: Yes, of course, Mr. Akimoto.

Hiroshi: Could you tell him that the new designs have arrived, and the first reactions are very positive.

Woman: Yes, I'll give him the message as soon as possible.

Hiroshi: Thank you very much. Goodbye.

Woman: Goodbye, Mr. Akimoto.

Phone call 2

Woman: ThaiWeb Designs. How can I help you?

Hiroshi: This is Hiroshi Akimoto from GameZ. I would like to speak to Anocha Thongdee.

Woman: I'm sorry, I didn't get your name. Could you repeat it, please?

Hiroshi: Hiroshi Akimoto from GameZ in Osaka.

Woman: Thank you, Mr. Akimoto. I'm afraid Ms. Thongdee is with a client. They are having lunch. Can I take a message?

Hiroshi: Thanks, but I need to talk to her about some designs she sent me. When is a good time for me to call her?

Woman: Oh, Ms. Thongdee will be back in the office in about an hour, so anytime after that would be fine.

Hiroshi: OK. Thanks. I'll call back later. Goodbye.

Phone call 3

Greg: Hello?

Hiroshi: Can I speak to Greg Murray, please?

Greg: Speaking.

Hiroshi: Hi, Greg. I didn't recognize your voice! I just wanted to ask you if you've seen the new designs from ThaiWeb Designs.

Greg: Yes, I'm looking at the new designs right now. They look good. What do you think?

Hiroshi: Yes, I like them, too. Let's have lunch together, and we can talk about them.

Greg: Good idea. See you in the cafeteria at one?

Hiroshi: OK. See you later. Bye.

Greg: Bye.

Track 13

1 Hi, Hiroshi. This is Greg. We want to meet for lunch today at one, but my boss needs to talk to me before he leaves the office at one-thirty. Could we have lunch earlier – let's say at twelve? Let me know if that's OK with you.

2 Good morning, Mr. Akimoto. This is James Neo from Singapore Software Systems. I'm calling about the new program designs. I am out of the office this morning, but can you call me back this afternoon?

3 Hiroshi, it's me, Takeshi. I need to talk to you. Can you meet me in front of my office this evening after work? Please call me back as soon as possible.

4 Hello, Mr. Akimoto. This is Christine Klein from Digital Design. We need to talk about my next trip to Osaka. Can you call me back, please?

5 Mr. Akimoto, this is James Neo again. I forgot to leave my cell phone number. From Japan you call 010 65 8653 1728.

6 Good morning, Mr. Akimoto. This is Miku Nomura from the Key Supply Company. I'm calling about the equipment you ordered. I'm afraid we can't send it until next month. Sorry about that.

Track 14

Interviewer:	Hi, what's your name?
Speaker 1:	Rozita.
Interviewer:	Could you spell that for me?
Speaker 1:	R-O-Z-I-T-A

Interviewer:	Hi, what's your name?
Speaker 2:	Yeonyi.
Interviewer:	How do you spell that?
Speaker 2:	Y-E-O-N-Y-I

Interviewer:	Hi, what's your name?
Speaker 3:	Shirley.
Interviewer:	Could you spell that for me?
Speaker 3:	S-H-I-R-L-E-Y

Interviewer:	Hi, what's your name?
Speaker 4:	Jerri.
Interviewer:	How do you spell that?
Speaker 4:	J-E-double R-I

Track 15

A for Alfa	**J** for Juliet	**S** for Sierra
B for Bravo	**K** for Kilo	**T** for Tango
C for Charlie	**L** for Lima	**U** for Uniform
D for Delta	**M** for Mike	**V** for Victor
E for Echo	**N** for November	**W** for Whiskey
F for Foxtrot	**O** for Oscar	**X** for X-ray
G for Golf	**P** for Papa	**Y** for Yankee
H for Hotel	**Q** for Quebec	**Z** for Zulu
I for India	**R** for Romeo	

Track 16

1
My name is Yori Sanada. That's Y-O-R-I S-A-N-A-D-A.

…

No, no. The first name is Yori. Y for Yankee, O for Oscar, R for Romeo, and I for India. The family name is S for Sierra, A for Alfa, N for November, A for Alfa, D for Delta, and A for Alfa.

2
This is Miku Nomura speaking, that's M-I-K-U and then N-O-M-U-R-A.

…

Yes, that's right. U for Uniform.

3
My name is Tom Robbins. Tom: Tango-Oscar-Mike; Robbins: Romeo-Oscar-Bravo-Bravo-India-November-Sierra.

…

Yes, that's right.

4
My last name is Vartak. I'll spell it for you: V-A-R-T-A-K. My first name is Paresh, P-A-R-E-S-H.

…

No, not B for Bravo. P for Papa. Paresh.

5
Jin Woong speaking. That's J-I-N and then W-double O-N-G.

…

No, no. Not G but J. J for Juliet.

…

No, let me give it to you again. My first name is Jin – J for Juliet, I for India, and N for November. My second name is Woong, that's Whiskey-Oscar-Oscar-November-Golf.

6
My name's Lopez, Quentin F. Lopez. Let me spell it for you. Q-U-E-N-T-I-N is my first name, then F for my middle initial, and my last name is L-O-P-E-Z: Quentin F. Lopez.

…

F for Foxtrot. My middle name is Frank. My full name is Quentin Frank Lopez.

Unit 4

Track 17

Conversation 1
Store clerk:	Do you need any help?
Customer:	Do you have any thumb drives?
Store clerk:	Yes. What size are you looking for?
Customer:	Well, um, I'm not sure. What do you have?
Store clerk:	We have some 32 gigabyte drives and a few 16 gigabyte drives left.
Customer:	Do you have any bigger ones?

Store clerk: No, sorry. We don't have any bigger drives, but we can order them for you.

Customer: What's the next size?

Store clerk: I can order 64 gigabytes. How many drives do you need?

Customer: Just one, thanks.

Conversation 2

Store clerk: Hello, how can I help you?

Customer: I'm looking for a gift for my girlfriend.

Store clerk: Well, how about a smartphone? We have some great smartphones.

Customer: No, she already has the latest smartphone. How much does a tablet cost?

Store clerk: Oh, they can be expensive, but we have some on sale for $300.

Customer: Do you have any tablets with Wi-Fi?

Store clerk: Oh, yes, all of them have Wi-Fi.

Customer: OK. Can I take a look at a $300 tablet, please?

Store clerk: Yes, of course.

Conversation 3

Customer: Excuse me. I wonder if you can help me. I want to download videos and watch them on my TV.

Store clerk: What kind of TV do you have?

Customer: It's one of the first HDTVs. It's my dad's.

Store clerk: What you need is a digital converter box that connects the Internet to your TV set.

Customer: Do you have any boxes that are not too expensive? I don't have much money.

Store clerk: Let me see, hmm. We don't have many, and they all cost over $100. We don't have any cheap ones left, but I'm expecting some tomorrow.

Customer: OK. I can come back tomorrow. No problem.

Track 18

Hi, I'm Liu and I love shopping. I usually spend all day Saturday with my friends at the shopping mall. We go from store to store and compare prices. We like to experiment with styles, so we try things on even if we can't afford to buy anything! We take breaks for coffee and ice cream, and it's a lot of fun. I never shop online because it's so boring. I like to see and feel things before I buy them. You can't see the real quality of a product on a computer screen. OK, you can send things back if you don't like them, or if they aren't the right size, but you need a lot of time to pack things up again and take them to the post office. And it's so easy to spend too much money when you can buy something with a click of the mouse!

Hi, I'm Huan. I'm an online shopper. I find shopping in a shopping mall really boring, and it can get really hectic and busy. You also waste a lot of time just to get there. Online shopping is much quicker. You can go from website to website much faster than you can go from store to store. You save money, too, because it's easy to compare prices and find the cheapest products. I buy everything online – even my clothes. I know the size and brand of jeans and trainers that are best for me, so I just order the same things every time I need some new stuff. I don't need to experiment – I know what I like. And when I want to buy some electronic equipment, there's better information online, and there are many more choices.

Track 19

A: Excuse me, are there any restrooms near here?

B: Yes. Go straight down this street. Turn right onto Main Street, then turn left onto Corn Street. Go straight for about 100 meters. The restrooms are on the right, next to the sushi bar and opposite the bookstore.

A: Thanks.

Track 20

When you get to the shopping mall, take the elevator to the second floor. The shoe store is opposite the elevator. Turn right. There's a pharmacy on the right, opposite the coffee shop. If you go straight, there's a small supermarket on the left, a sports store on the right, and a Vietnamese restaurant after that. But don't go straight. Turn right and you will see Alta Moda. There's a cell phone store on your right and a furniture store on your left.

Track 21

1
A The man is laughing.
B The man is in the park.
C The man isn't happy.
D The man is using a cell phone.

2
A The boy is holding some books.
B The boy and girl are in the supermarket.
C The girl is helping the boy.
D The boy is helping the girl.

Track 22

Conversation 1
Woman 1: Good morning. How can I help you?
Woman 2: Do you have this blue top in any other color?
Woman 1: Yes, we have it in green.
Woman 2: Oh, I like green. How much does it cost?
Woman 1: It costs $30.
Woman 2: That's expensive. I can't afford that!
Woman 1: Well, we have some green T-shirts. They cost $15.
Woman 2: OK. A green T-shirt, please, in medium.

Question 1 What does the green top cost?
Question 2 Which statement is correct?
Question 3 What does the woman buy?

Conversation 2
Woman: Hello. This is Mia Johnson. I'd like to come in on Thursday or Friday. When is Carlo free?
Man: I'll just check the calendar. Hmm, yes, he's free on Friday, Ms. Johnson. Wash and cut at three o'clock, or is four better?
Woman: Four is perfect. Thanks. Bye.

Question 1 Who is the woman calling?
Question 2 Why is the woman calling?
Question 3 When will the woman see Carlo?

Unit 5

Track 23

John: John Santos, Greencheck Software. How can I help you?
Mr. Parks: Can I speak to Dr. Little, please? My name's David Parks. Dr. Little and I were in Hong Kong at a conference last week. This week I'm in Manila. Dr. Little is expecting my call.
John: I'm sorry, Mr. Parks. He's in a meeting right now, but he wants me to make an appointment with you.
Mr. Parks: Fine. Can you make a suggestion?
John: Let me see, mmm, today's Tuesday. Is later today possible?
Mr. Parks: No, sorry. I'm having lunch with a client at one o'clock, and later today I'm attending a workshop. What about tomorrow?
John: I'm sorry. Dr. Little has a lot of meetings on Wednesday. Let's look at Thursday.
Mr. Parks: No, no. On Thursday I'm meeting some clients. What about the day after?
John: Friday is no problem. What's better for you, the morning or the afternoon?
Mr. Parks: The morning is better for me.
John: Well, why don't you come late morning, Mr. Parks? Then you can have lunch with Dr. Little.
Mr. Parks: That's a good idea. Shall we say eleven-thirty?
John: Fine. Friday at eleven-thirty. Thank you for your call. Goodbye.

Track 24

Lien: OK, Ken. Let's check the plans for SuperAsia's new CD. I'm having a meeting with the band's agent this Friday. We're meeting at the Royal Hotel at 2 PM.
Ken: Would it be possible for me to come, too?
Lien: It's not really necessary, Ken. We only need to discuss one or two details. They're coming here to the office next Tuesday afternoon at 5 PM to sign the contract. Then we all go out to dinner. Any idea where we could go?

Ken: What about trying that new restaurant on Wellington Street. I think it's called Amigo.

Lien: Good idea. Why don't you book a table for eight at 7 PM? You're coming, too, of course, Huan?

Huan: Sure, Lien. But don't forget we are recording early on Wednesday. We start at eight and we don't want the boys to be too tired. We only have ten days in the studio, so every day is important if we want to have the album before Christmas.

Lien: OK. Let's make sure they're back in their hotel before ten. Next point: What about the CD cover design, Ken?

Ken: I'm meeting with the designer next Friday. She's bringing some cover designs with her, so we can choose the one we like best.

Lien: Good. When we have the final design, we can start the promotion campaign. Should we have a meeting about that the day after tomorrow? Let's say Thursday at 10 AM?

Ken: Fine.

Lien: OK, I have to go. I need to prepare for the presentation I'm giving tomorrow.

Track 25

Monday, Tuesday, Wednesday, Thursday, Friday, Saturday, Sunday

Track 26

January, February, March, April, May, June, July, August, September, October, November, December

Track 27

July 2nd, 2010; August 3rd, 1996; December 25th, 1945; February 11th, 1966

Track 28

1 **A:** Does the product come onto the market on June 1st?
  B: No, on July 1st.

2 **A:** Are you flying to Tokyo on Monday?
  B: No, I'm flying on Tuesday, and the meeting is on Wednesday.

3 **A:** Your birthday is in February, isn't it?
  B: No, it's on March 22nd.

4 **A:** When is the next workshop?
  B: It's on October 30th.

Track 29

1 It's twenty-five to eight in the morning.
2 It's a quarter to three in the afternoon.
3 It's twenty to seven in the evening.
4 It's half past three in the afternoon.
5 It's a quarter past eleven in the morning.
6 It's half past five in the morning.
7 It's seven o'clock in the evening.
8 It's twenty past eight in the morning.
9 It's a quarter to nine in the evening.
10 It's noon.

Track 30

Hello. My name is Millie Dresser. I come from Australia, but I work in Germany and China. Today I want to talk to you about different styles of communication in those countries.

Take, for example, the word "no." If you ask people in Germany "Can you help me?" they will often just say "No." In my country, it's usual to add something, like "No, I'm sorry, I can't." But many Asians try not to use the word "no" at all. They don't want the other person to feel uncomfortable. In China it's important to watch a person's body language. This can help you to understand what people there really mean.

Germans generally have a very direct communication style. This can surprise or upset people from other cultures. Germans can also be very formal when they do business. They don't often use first names with colleagues or business partners. In China businesspeople are also very formal, so it's best to use their last name and their title. Say, for example, "Good morning, Chief Engineer Chen." But here in Australia, we are often informal with our business partners and very quickly use first names.

In meetings in my country we often interrupt people. Of course, we try to do it politely. The Germans interrupt a lot and sometimes shout! In China you must never shout or interrupt people in meetings. You have to show respect for your colleagues at all times.

Before we do business in Australia, we usually make small talk. They do the same in China. But not in Germany. The Germans don't usually like small talk at meetings. They prefer to talk about what they are there for – business!

Another interesting thing is how different nationalities feel about teamwork. In many Asian countries, including China, people like working in teams. We Australians are good at teamwork, too. But in some northern European countries, such as Germany and Finland, people often prefer to work alone.

Well, these are just a few of the things I have seen on my business travels. I hope my tips are useful.

Unit 6

Track 31

Conversation 1

Lucy: The Plaza Hotel. How can I help you?

Caller 1: Hello. My name is Jenny Bond. I have a reservation for a single room for three nights in March. From the nineteenth to the twenty-first, leaving on the twenty-second.

Lucy: That's right, Ms. Bond. I have your reservation here.

Caller 1: Yes, well I would like to stay for two more nights and leave on the twenty-fourth. Is that possible?

Lucy: Let me see . . . mmm . . . oh, I'm sorry, we don't have a single room on those dates. I can offer you a double room. The double room is bigger and more comfortable than a single room, but of course, it's more expensive.

Caller 1: How much does it cost?

Lucy: Well, I can give you one of our most expensive rooms at a special price for the five nights. That would be $600. It's one of our biggest rooms, and it's very comfortable.

Caller 1: Well, it's very expensive, but OK. Can you confirm the reservation by email, please?

Lucy: Yes, of course, Ms. Bond. We have your email address here.

Caller: Thank you very much. Goodbye.

Conversation 2

Lucy: Good morning. The Plaza Hotel. How can I help you?

Caller 2: Good morning. My name is Anton Wijaya. I have two reservations for this Friday, leaving Sunday. One is for me and one is for Dr. Little.

Lucy: Just one moment, Mr. Wijaya, let me just check that. Yes, I have it here. Arriving Friday the fourteenth for two nights. Is there a problem?

Caller 2: Not really. It's just that I've changed my plans, and I'm taking a later flight. We land at 10 PM, so I can't be at the hotel before midnight.

Lucy: That's not a problem, Mr. Wijaya. We have someone at reception twenty-four hours a day.

Caller 2: Oh, that's good. I can take a taxi from the airport, so I expect to arrive at twelve-thirty at the latest.

Lucy: That's fine, Mr. Wijaya. I can inform my colleagues of your late arrival.

Caller 2: Thanks a lot. By the way, Dr. Little's flight is not as late as mine. He'll be there earlier than me.

Lucy: OK. Well, have a good flight, Mr. Wijaya.

Track 32

Tony: How was your trip to Bangkok, Sinittra?

Sinittra: It was great. I really like flying. You're going to the Bangkok office next week, aren't you, Tony? I'm sure you'll enjoy the trip, too.

Tony: Oh, I'm not so sure. It's a very long trip, and it's my first long-haul flight. You travel a lot, Sinittra. Do you have any advice for me?

Sinittra: Well, I have some rules for myself that make the trip easier. For example, I always go to bed early the night before. On the day of the trip itself I only have light meals. And I always leave for the airport early. It's better to have too much time than too little.

Tony: OK. What about clothes? What should I wear?

Sinittra: Wear something loose and comfortable. And always have a warm pullover in your carry-on luggage. You can quickly feel cold when you're tired.

Tony: What about alcohol? I often feel nervous when I fly, and a beer or two helps.

Sinittra: Not a good idea, Tony. It's better to drink juice and water. And drink as much as you can. To relax watch a movie, play computer games, or talk to other people. And don't forget to stand up and move around during the flight. That's very important on a long-haul flight.

Tony: OK. That's great, Sinittra. Thanks so much for your advice.

Sinittra: You're welcome. And have a good flight!

Track 33

Clerk: The Richmond Hotel. How can I help you?

Caller: Hello. My name is Emma Sari. I have a reservation for a single room for three nights in July. From the first to the third, leaving on the fourth.

Clerk: Yes, that's right, Ms. Sari. I have your reservation here.

Caller: Yes, well, I'd like to stay longer and leave on the seventh. Is that possible?

Clerk: Let me see . . . mmm . . . that's three more nights. Oh, I'm sorry, we don't have a single room available on those dates. But I can offer you a double room at a special price for the six nights.

Caller: How much would that be?

Clerk: That would be $900 in total.

Caller: OK, that's fine. Can you confirm the reservation by email, please?

Clerk: Yes, of course, Ms. Sari. We have your email address here.

Caller: Thank you very much. Goodbye.

Track 34

1
A The receptionist is shaking the guest's hand.
B The hotel guest is paying by credit card.
C The hotel guest is filling out a form.
D The receptionist is making a phone call.

2
A The motorist is driving on the highway.
B The police officer is laughing at the motorist.
C The motorist is shouting at the police officer.
D The police officer is writing a ticket.

Track 35

Good morning, ladies and gentlemen, and welcome to New York. My name is Sandra, and I'm your guide. We will begin today's tour with a visit to Ground Zero. There I will tell you more about the 9/11 attack on the World Trade Center. After that we will have a one-hour lunch break in the Boathouse Restaurant in Central Park. After lunch you will have one-and-a-half hours to take a walk in the park. At three-thirty we will all meet outside the Central Park Zoo. Then you can either visit the zoo, or you can come with me to the Dakota building. This is the building where John Lennon lived with his wife Yoko Ono. He was shot there in 1980. The Strawberry Fields Park is nearby. It was named after one of the Beatles' most famous songs. OK, let's go.

Track 36

Imagine you work at the reception desk of a hotel in the centre of your city. A hotel guest is asking you for information about your city.

Question 1 What are the hours of the stores here? (Beep)

Question 2 What are the best places to visit on foot? (Beep)

Question 3 Are there any good restaurants nearby? (Beep)

Unit 7

Track 37

Interviewer: Good morning, listeners. On our program today, our special guest is fashion designer Lee-kyung Kim. Good morning, Lee-kyung.

Lee-kyung: Good morning.

Interviewer: Lee-kyung, your company LKK Fashions is in Seoul. Were you born in Seoul?

Lee-kyung: Yes, in 1985. After school, I studied fashion design at the university there.

Interviewer: And what did you do after you left university?

Lee-kyung: I went to France to study in Paris. That was in 2007.

Interviewer: And when did you get the idea to start your own company?

Lee-kyung: Well, I got the idea while I was in France, but I didn't have enough money or experience.

Interviewer: And why did you leave France?

Lee-kyung: I wasn't really happy there, so I returned to Korea at the beginning of 2009. I worked for a film company in Busan for two years. I designed costumes for movies. I got a lot of experience and saved a lot of money. It was a great job.

Interviewer: So why didn't you stay there?

Lee-kyung: I didn't want to work for a large company any longer. I wanted to work for myself, so in 2011 I moved back to Seoul and started LKK Fashions.

Interviewer: You were only 26 years old!

Lee-kyung: Yes, but we were very successful.

Interviewer: When did you decide to specialize in men's fashion?

Lee-kyung: That was in 2013. And last year our New Man fashion show in Sydney, Australia, won the Australian Fashion Award. I didn't expect to win, and I was very proud.

Interviewer: That's great, Lee-kyung. I wish you and your company lots of success in the future.

Track 38

The Lenovo Group is a Chinese company that makes computer hardware. Lenovo started in Beijing in 1984. Its first successful product was the Han-card. This card made it possible to use Chinese characters on personal computers. Today Lenovo has 27,000 employees and sells its products in around 160 countries. Its revenue is about 30 billion US dollars a year. The company's headquarters are in North Carolina in the United States.

The Hyundai Motor Company is the world's fourth largest automobile producer. It started in 1967 in Seoul, South Korea, where the company headquarters are still located today. In 1986 Hyundai began to sell cars in the United States. Today they sell vehicles in 193 different countries. The company has about 75,000 employees worldwide. Its revenue is about 76 billion US dollars every year.

Olam International Limited is a global food company with over 12,000 customers worldwide. The company started in West Africa in 1989. It moved its headquarters to Singapore in 1995. Today Olam deals with 20 different products from many different countries. The company has about 18,000 employees in 65 countries worldwide. Company revenue is about 14 billion US dollars each year.

Asian Paints is one of the largest paint companies in the world with revenue of 1.9 billion US dollars. Four friends started the company in 1942 in Bombay, India. By 1967 it was India's leading paint company. Today it has 5,000 employees and is in 17 countries. Its headquarters are still in Bombay, which today, of course, is called Mumbai.

Track 39

1

My name is Sylvia Astengo. I'm a fashion designer and I'm from Italy. I work a lot in China. On my last trip to Shanghai, my business partners took me out to dinner. There was an accident at the table. The waiter dropped some food on my dress. I was really angry and shouted at him to be more careful. Everyone at the table was quiet. I think I did something wrong.

2

I'm Michael Gomez and I'm from Manila in the Philippines. For Filipinos it's normal to ask someone how old they are. When I was on a business trip in Toronto, Canada, there was a female boss. We had lunch together. I told her I was twenty-eight. Then I asked her her age. The other people at the table got very red faces.

3

Hi. I'm Ryan Forbes. I'm from Los Angeles in the United States. I'm a computer network specialist. Last week I was on a business trip in Liverpool in the UK. My job was to train the employees to use a new system. Well, one day during lunch I asked them how much they earn in their jobs. They looked very uncomfortable. Did I do something wrong?

4

Hello. I'm Sandra Miles. My company sent me to Vietnam on business. The people there are really nice and friendly. But I think I did something wrong. I told my business partners that I think our government here in the UK is not very good. They looked really shocked!

5

My name is Adi Kurniawan and I work for a big electronics company in Indonesia. I often do business in Saudi Arabia. My business trips are usually a success, but there's one thing I don't understand. When I meet my business partners, I always ask them about their wives and families – the way we do in my country. They don't answer my questions. Am I doing something wrong?

Unit 8

Track 40

Conversation 1

Marc: Hello. This is Marc Simpson.

Amy: Hi, Marc. It's Amy, Amy Anderson. How are you?

Marc: Oh, hi, Amy. Well, I'm really busy, but things are good.

Amy: I hope you're not too busy, Marc. You mustn't leave Singapore before we've a chance to meet. That's why I'm calling – I'd like to invite you to lunch.

Marc: Thanks for the invitation, Amy. Yes, we must meet for lunch. Where?

Amy: There's a new Italian restaurant near my office. Everyone says it's great and we have had to try it. What about tomorrow? Are you free?

Marc: I'm afraid I can't come tomorrow. Wednesday is better for me. I can come on Wednesday.

Amy: OK. Wednesday is good for me, too. What about twelve-thirty? We can meet here, at my office. Does that suit you?

Marc: Fine. See you at your office at twelve-thirty on Wednesday.

Conversation 2

Man: Restaurant La Vita, how can I help you?

Amy: Good morning. My name is Anderson, Amy Anderson. Can I reserve a table for two?

Man: For this evening?

Amy: No, no. For lunch on Wednesday.

Man: Oh, you don't need to reserve a table for lunch. We're never very busy at lunchtime. But you have to make a reservation if you want to come in the evening.

Amy: I see. OK. No, it's just for lunch, thanks. Bye.

Man: Bye.

Conversation 3

Amy: Oh, the menu is in Italian. Do you speak Italian, Marc?

Marc: No, I don't speak it, but I can understand quite a lot.

Amy: Me too. Mmm, pasta with salmon sounds good.

Marc: Or the chicken risotto. Yes, that's it. Chicken risotto with salad.

Amy: What are you having to drink?

Marc: Mineral water is fine.

Amy: Yes, a glass of mineral water for me, too.

Marc: So, Amy, let's get down to business. I only have an hour and a half. I have a meeting at two o'clock, and I mustn't be late.

Amy: OK. Waiter, can you take our order, please?

Track 41

Tony: Well, this is interesting. I've never been to a food court before.

Chermarn: Oh, food courts are really popular here in Bangkok. And you can get really great Thai dishes here. Now what would you like to eat?

Tony: There's so much to choose from. What do you recommend?

Chermarn: They have a really good *tom yam* here. You can have it with shrimp or with chicken.

Tony: Oh, that's a bit too spicy for me.

Chermarn: What about *pad Thai*?

Tony: I don't know what that is. Can you explain it to me?

Chermarn: It's noodles with a special sauce with peanuts, egg, and bean sprouts. You can have it with pork, chicken, seafood, or tofu.

Tony: That sounds good. I'll have that. What are you having?

Chermarn: The *tom yam* for me. And afterwards we can have something sweet for dessert.

Tony: Great. What's that over there?

Chermarn: That's mango with sticky rice. It comes with coconut milk.

Tony: Wow. Delicious! It's a good thing I'm not on a diet today!

Track 42

Example: When did you last see Mai?
- **A** She lives in London.
- **B** She visited me yesterday.
- **C** Probably next week.

1 Excuse me. Is there a supermarket near here?
- **A** No, it's not there.
- **B** Yes. It's next to the bank.
- **C** Yes, can I help you?

2 Where do you usually have lunch?
- **A** Oh, I never have lunch.
- **B** It's usually about midday.
- **C** The sushi bar isn't open at lunchtime.

3 Can I reserve a single room?
- **A** The train leaves from platform two.
- **B** For how many nights?
- **C** The hotel has a restaurant.

4 Would you like to have dinner with me?
- **A** Can I have the check, please?
- **B** I enjoyed the meal.
- **C** I'm afraid I can't.

Track 43

Conversation 1

Man: Good morning, Sandy. How are things?

Woman: OK, Mike. Are you going to the meeting with us after lunch?

Man: No. I'm leaving early today. I'm taking my son to the dentist this afternoon.

Question 1 Who are the speakers?

Question 2 Where are they having the conversation?

Question 3 What's Sandy planning to do?

Conversation 2

Woman: Good morning. How can I help you?

Man: I reserved a double room for my wife and me for three nights June 1st to 3rd. The name's Tomlin. T-O-M-L-I-N.

Woman: Just a moment. Let me check. Hmm, I'm afraid we don't have a reservation under that name in our computer, sir. Did we send you written confirmation?

Question 1 Where are the speakers?

Question 2 When are the Tomlins leaving?

Question 3 What's the problem?

Unit 9

Track 44

Amsyar: What do you like best about your job, Ly?

Ly: Well, I like meeting people, and I enjoy talking to customers. What about you?

Amsyar: My job's interesting, and I like working with the colleagues in my department. They're really nice, and I enjoy working in a team.

Ly: That's great, but there has to be something you don't like.

Amsyar: Well, I really dislike going to conferences because they're usually a waste of time.

Ly: Oh, I don't mind going to conferences, but I hate giving presentations. I'm always so nervous.

Amsyar: Me, too. What about reports? I hate reading reports. They can be so boring.

Ly: I know what you mean. And I dislike writing them, too. That can be really difficult. But I don't mind looking after visitors. That's often fun!

Track (45)

Ly: What about after work, Amsyar? How do you spend your leisure time?

Amsyar: Well, I work long hours, so I don't have much free time. I prefer to spend it with my family. What about you?

Ly: Well, I'm learning to play the saxophone.

Amsyar: Really?

Ly: And I try to do as many sports as I can. I need to spend a lot of time in the gym if I want to stay fit. Do you do any sports?

Amsyar: No, not really. I prefer to watch sports on TV!

Ly: Oh, Amsyar, you're so lazy! Well, I enjoyed talking, but now I have to go. I promised to write a report, and I want to finish it today.

Amsyar: OK, Ly. I hope to see you at lunch again tomorrow.

Track (46)

Interviewer: Welcome to our program about the travel and leisure industry in Asia. First we would like to welcome Lillian Majid from International Leisure Services. Ms. Majid, tell us something about your company.

Ms. Majid: Good morning everyone. International Leisure Services is located in Kuala Lumpur. We plan and develop health spas, golf clubs, and theme parks.

Interviewer: And where are your main activities?

Ms. Majid: We're now active in eight different countries in the region, mainly in China, Thailand, and Indonesia.

Interviewer: And how are the countries different?

Ms. Majid: Well, Thailand is the spa capital of Asia. There are thousands of spas, and visitors come from all over the world to do something for their health. In China the golf industry is very important, and it's growing very fast. In fact, we expect 20 million players in China by 2020. Today many golfers from Australia and Japan prefer to play golf in China because it's much cheaper.

Interviewer: What about theme parks?

Ms. Majid: There are some great theme parks all over the region, especially in Indonesia. My company built a fantastic water park last year on Bali, right in the middle of a tropical park. People not only enjoy swimming there, they can also take part in games and entertainment. And for those who like eating and drinking, there are several restaurants and bars. It's a wonderful place for young and old.

Interviewer: And what about your company's future?

Majid: The travel and leisure industry is a trillion-dollar industry worldwide, and it's still growing. So I'm sure my company will have a lot to do in the future.

Interviewer: Thank you very much, Ms. Majid.

Track (47)

Dan: What do you do in your free time, Emma?

Emma: Well, I'm learning to play the guitar, and I have to practice every day. On the weekends I go shopping. To stay fit I do aerobics. In the summer

I go backpacking and in the winter I go skiing. Do you do any sports, Dan?

Dan: Oh, yes. I do a lot of sports. I go swimming every morning, and after work I do weight training. On the weekend I do karate. I'm in a club. And sometimes I play soccer. I'd like to learn to play golf, but it's too expensive.

Emma: Do you like to go jogging? I really hate it.

Dan: Oh, I don't mind jogging. But I don't like to go cycling.

Emma: Oh, really. I like to go cycling. Do you play any games?

Dan: Yes, I play computer games and sometimes I play chess with my dad. He's really good.

Unit 10

Track 48

Chermarn: What time is your flight, Tony?

Tony: At half past six this evening.

Chermarn: And when will you arrive home?

Tony: We'll land at about a quarter to seven tomorrow morning. I hope we won't be late. I'll take a taxi from the airport, and I'll be home about nine o'clock.

Chermarn: Oh, that's a long trip.

Tony: It's no problem. I won't sleep much, but I'll read and play computer games.

Chermarn: Well. Tony, it was nice to meet you.

Tony: It was a pleasure for me, too, Chermarn.

Chermarn: I hope you'll visit us again soon.

Tony: Me, too. And thanks for all your help. I hope you'll accept this small gift.

Chermarn: Oh, that's very kind of you, Tony. May I open it now?

Tony: Sure, go ahead.

Chermarn: Oh, it's a book about Sydney. I'd love to go to Sydney.

Tony: Well, then, I hope our next meeting will be in Sydney.

Chermarn: That would be wonderful. Please give my regards to your colleagues.

Tony: Yes, Chermarn, I'll do that.

Chermarn: Well, goodbye. Have a good trip home. And please come again soon!

Tony: I definitely will, Chermarn. Goodbye. I'll be in touch.

Track 49

Sora Kim: My name is Sora Kim, and I'd like to welcome you to our program. Today I'm talking to Chen Ming about his book *The 2025 Workplace*. Chen, tell us what the book is about.

Chen Ming: Well, in the past people went to their workplace. Then new technologies came and made it possible to work from home – what we call "remote working."

Sora Kim: And in the future?

Chen Ming: In the future work will be even more flexible and mobile. We will work anywhere we choose. In fact, there probably won't be any offices. All our workplaces will be virtual.

Sora Kim: What does that mean?

Chen Ming: For example, employees will work together on projects but live in places with thousands of miles between them.

Sora Kim: How will they do that?

Chen Ming: With cell phones, special touch screens, and wooosh! – there you are in the company's virtual office.

Sora Kim: So you won't actually meet your colleagues?

Chen Ming: That's right. With new technologies it will be possible to have web-conferences with 3D avatars. Nobody can see who you really are, where you are, or how you look. So you can wear your pajamas at home in your living room and take part in an important business conference!

Sora Kim: Wow. That's fantastic! But won't it be expensive?

Chen Ming: Yes, but companies won't spend money on offices and equipment or on travel costs for business trips.

Sora Kim:	But does it mean we'll be at work 24/7?
Chen Ming:	That depends on you. The good thing about the online society of the future is that it will have an off-button. That's why it's so attractive.

Track 50

Sanda Myint

I like my job, so I'll definitely stay with this company for as long as I can. The company also has an office in the United States, so I'll probably work there for a year or two, but I'll definitely come back to Myanmar. I'll probably get married and have children one day, but I definitely want to continue working after I'm married.

Saiful Muhamat

I definitely want to travel. My company is growing, so I'll probably travel to Europe some time in the next few years. If I do, I'll definitely take my family with me. Later I'll probably study some more and get a better degree – perhaps an MBA.

Track 51

1
A   The shopper is trying on some clothes.
B   The shopper is reading something on the bottle.
C   The shopper is wearing a thick pullover.
D   The shopper is paying for her shopping at the register.

2
A   The couple is walking in a busy street.
B   The couple is walking in the park on a spring day.
C   The couple is sitting under the trees.
D   The couple is carrying umbrellas.

Track 52

Hi, this is Sandy James. I'd like to leave a message for Eddie Johnson.
It's about two on Friday afternoon. We have an appointment for a meeting with Tony Marshall on Monday morning. Well, I'm really sorry, Eddie, but I can't make it. But I hope we can still have the meeting next week. I'm available on Wednesday and Thursday, and I'm pretty flexible on those days, although Wednesday is better for me. So could you decide what suits you best and find out from Tony if he can make it on one of those days? We can meet at my office as we planned – or at your office if that suits you better.
I'm sorry for the late cancellation. Please call me as soon as you hear this message. You can reach me on my cell phone 0162 24689, or you can call my office at 5469872 and leave a message with my secretary. She'll be in the office until 5 PM today. Thanks, Eddie. Hope to hear from you soon.

Credits

The publisher would like to thank the following for permission to reproduce photographs and illustrations (key: left to right, top to bottom):